THE UNWEPT

The Unwept

Black American Soldiers and
the Spanish-American War

Edward Van Zile Scott

The Black Belt Press
Montgomery

The Black Belt Press

P.O. Box 551

Montgomery, AL 36101

A Rivendell Press Book

Publishers Cataloging in Publication Data

Scott, Edward Van Zile, 1921-
    The Unwept: Black American Soldiers and the Spanish-Ameri-
    can War / by Edward Van Zile Scott
       p.   cm.
    ISBN 1-881320-62-6
    1. Soldiers-U.S. 2. African American-History. I. Title.
    1996

                                              CIP

99 98 97 96   5 4 3 2 1

*The Black Belt, defined by its dark, rich soil, stretches across central
Alabama. It was the heart of the cotton belt. It was and is a place
of great beauty, of extreme wealth and grinding poverty, of pain
and joy. Here we take our stand, listening to the past, looking to the
future.*

Dedicated to the Memory of

Walter Seymore Scott

Contents

Table of Military Units

Black Units:

Ninth Cavalry
Tenth Cavalry
Twenty-Fourth Infantry
Twenty-Fifth Infantry

White Units:

First Cavalry
First Infantry
First U.S. Volunteer Cavalry
Fourth Infantry
Second Georgia Volunteer Infantry
Second Infantry
Second Massachusetts Volunteer Infantry
Seventeenth Infantry
Seventy-first New York Volunteer Infantry
Signal Corps
Sixth Cavalry
Third Cavalry
Thirteenth Infantry
Twelfth Infantry

PREFACE

Military artifacts played far more than an incidental role in my young life, as much a part of my childhood as the early morning freight trains announcing the beginning of commerce each day or the late afternoon sunsets which, through a haze of steel-making and industry, would frame the city each evening in a spectacular display of color. In our family's large three-story house overlooking Birmingham, Alabama, one would find— hanging on the walls of the room somewhat extravagantly called the library—Indian moccasins and ceremonial beadwork, and, certainly more menacing, warriors' bows and the arrows that accompanied them. Next to an elaborately decorated tomahawk were the most gruesome artifacts: two full-length Indian war bonnets, each plume representing victory over an opponent in battle, and on whose feathers were attached pieces of dried human scalp.

An exotic element of the Far East rounded out the collection. Moro spears from the Philippines, five feet or more in length, were tipped with intricately etched yet quite lethal points. Eclectically mixed in with this display were several pairs of minuscule Chinese shoes, so very small it seemed they could not possibly have fit an adult foot. I was told these shoes had actually been worn by Chinese ladies whose feet had been tightly bound from early childhood to make them conform to the small size of the shoe. I was not thoroughly convinced at the time, and, although

I have since learned it to be true, I still have a hard time comprehending such a brutal practice.

All these military and cultural relics had been collected over the years by my paternal grandfather, Colonel Walter S. Scott, an infantry officer in the United States Army. This mysterious grandfather, who appeared at rare intervals throughout my childhood, was a solemn, taciturn man, in all likelihood overwhelmed by my parents' boisterous offspring—out of eight children I was the second of four boys. No tales of sweaty campaigns or Indian ambushes could be prodded from this tight-lipped old warrior. How must he have felt after days and frequently weeks of relentless pursuit to have finally engaged the Indians in battle, in territory that the Indians knew intimately— it was *their* land, wasn't it, after all—and against numbers vastly superior? How must he have felt to have had deadly bullets ripping through the bushes by his side in Cuba? Had he ever had to dodge a Moro spear in the Philippines? As children, we were only left to imagine.

This exposure to things military and things exotic, coupled with the mystery of my grandfather's past, forged my early interest in history. It is an interest I have pursued and nurtured throughout my life, spanning the many years of my marriage and my medical practice. When I retired several years ago, I decided to research my grandfather's story and to inquire into the details of his military career; I then spent several years compiling and exploring the facts of his life and his times.

My research led me to a very interesting pass. I was surprised to learn that during most of his career my grandfather led black infantry troops, not white soldiers. I cannot speculate as to why my grandfather chose to give up a teaching career to join the Army. After being accepted to the military academy at West Point, he decided to pass up the opportunity. He elected to forgo a West Point education and the preferred officer status that would have followed, and instead accepted the army's offer to become an instant second lieutenant. Did he know that part of the deal was assignment to a black infantry outfit? I suspect that his posting to the Twenty-fifth Infantry, where he faithfully served for many years, came after he had been sworn in as a second lieutenant.

In any case, I was even more surprised to learn that black soldiers of that time constituted a significant portion of the regular Army ranks and played a substantial and often crucial role in many battles. Most surprising of all was that in the Spanish-American War of 1898, veteran black troops—some under command of Captain Walter S. Scott of the Twenty-fifth Infantry—were more responsible than any other group for the United States' victory.

What I have uncovered in setting out to understand my grandfather's life is a most remarkable fact, a fact left out of our shared American history: A relatively small number of black soldiers (about 13 percent of the attacking forces), most of them veterans of campaigns in the West, were essential to defeating the Spanish and bringing the war to a quick conclusion.

In none of my studies during public school in Birmingham, preparatory school in Virginia, or college at the University of Virginia in Charlottesville had I encountered these facts. Although I am not a professional historian, when I uncovered the extent of the black soldiers' participation in this chapter of American history—a participation that I subsequently learned has not been properly emphasized—I knew this was a story that I must tell.

Perhaps historians have underplayed the black soldier's vital role because of poor reporting during the war. Accurate reporting of a distant war that lasted only thirteen hours of actual fighting was difficult in those pre-CNN days, and many newspaper accounts at the time, as well as later historical writings, were based on quite restricted, secondary sources. Perhaps the historical record was also obscured because of violent racial conflicts immediately preceding and for many years after the war. Many contemporary accounts certainly were plainly and deliberately biased.

Whatever the reason for the shortcomings of earlier accounts of the Spanish-American War, truth has been the victim, and it is the intention of this history to set the record as straight as I can under the circumstances. My own documentation, limited by time and distance, has had to come from a variety of primary and secondary sources: autobiographies of those present, information from military records, and letters written by soldiers who fought in the battles.

THE UNWEPT

Photos of black U.S. soldiers of the Spanish-American War are rare. The top photo on this page, which also appears on the cover of this book, shows enlisted men of the U.S. Tenth Cavalry following the capture of San Juan Hill, July 1898. The bottom photo, from the Library of Congress, shows Troop K of the Tenth. Similar photos in the National Archives also depict Troops A through M of the Tenth. The photo on the opposite page was provided to the author by Booker T. Brooks, of Washington, D.C., the fifth son of veteran William Prince Brooks, who is standing at the far right on the back row. Mr. Brooks is a member of the "Buffalo Soldiers," an

organization of descendants of veterans and other interested persons. He also provided a copy of some of his father's service records, and the following interpretation of the photo: *"It is not known when or where this photograph was taken. It is believed that it was taken sometime during the enlistment of William Prince Brooks during the period from May 24, 1898, to May 23, 1901. The non-commissioned officer stripe of private first class appears on the sleeve of the soldier seated second from the left. It is possible that this is a photo of the non-commissioned officers of Troop G, [Ninth U.S. Cavalry]. The only person known by me in this photograph is William Prince Brooks... born in Cabarrus County, North Carolina... October 21, 1878. He enlisted while enrolled at Tuskegee Institute studying to be a wheelwright. Records show he was [nineteen] years of age at the time of his enlistment... Records show that William Prince Brooks was promoted to Corporal on January 18, 1899 [and that he also] participated in engagements and actions in the Philippine Islands from September 16, 1900, to May 23, 1901."* Corporal William Prince Brooks died August 3, 1969, in Washington, D.C., and is buried there at the U.S. Soldiers Home Cemetery.

INTRODUCTION

When I began to research the life of my grandfather, Colonel Walter S. Scott, the last decade of the nineteenth century was to me hardly more than a footnote in history. Although it was not that long ago—I was born just twenty-three years after the end of the Spanish-American War—it is a time that has largely been forgotten or rather eclipsed by the turmoil of the early 1900s and the convulsions of the ensuing modern era. It is a time that is conspicuously absent from many of our textbooks. And it is a time lost in our collective memory. The 1890s were nonetheless a crucial decade—a turning point for the United States and Spain.

Given the tendency of historical events to be obliterated by the passage of time and the encroachment of ever more recent events, it is not surprising that most Americans know only two facts about the Spanish-American War: first, an explosion caused the battleship *Maine* to sink in the harbor of Havana, and second, Theodore Roosevelt led the Rough Riders in a heroic charge up San Juan Hill. Few Americans are aware, however, that because of its long-term consequences, the Spanish-American War was one of the world's decisive struggles. American defeat— or even a stalemate—would have radically altered the history of the twentieth century, with isolationism more than likely dominating American foreign policy for many years after the war.

I was also surprised to learn of the brief duration of the actual fighting. The three land battles of the Spanish-American War *in total* lasted a mere thirteen hours. Because the war was so brief, most Americans have understandably failed to appreciate its significance as a watershed in modern history.

Relatively little is known about the brave men of the two black cavalry and the two black infantry regiments, who, to this day, have not received their due for this victory. The highly publicized actions of Teddy Roosevelt and his volunteer troops, who comprised only 3 percent of the attacking forces, are about the only details known by most Americans, while the courageous efforts of the black troops in the war have slipped from history.

This oversight of valiant and patriotic men is especially poignant considering the circumstances under which the black soldiers served their nation.

The black component of the United States Army in the second half of the nineteenth century consisted of four regiments, the Ninth Cavalry and Tenth Cavalry, and the Twenty-fourth Infantry and Twenty-fifth Infantry. These regiments had been formed shortly after the Civil War, drawing troops from some two hundred thousand black Union soldiers discharged at war's end.

Almost without exception, the black soldiers had been stationed in the less populated region of the country west of the Mississippi. Among the inequities and injustices that plagued them were inferior supplies. It was common knowledge that black outfits received more or less what was left after whites had been equipped—the sick, decrepit horses that had been rejected by white cavalry units, grossly inadequate rations, and deteriorating, outmoded equipment. (However, by 1898, even black regulars had been furnished the new smokeless-powder Krag-Jorgensen rifle[1] that later proved to be very effective in their trained hands during the Spanish-American War, to the immediate benefit of an ill-prepared Teddy Roosevelt.)

The army promoted blacks to officer status only on the rarest of occasions, so black troops were inevitably led by white officers—between 1866 and 1898 all but three line officers of black troops were white. Even the white officers so assigned were likely prejudiced against serving with black troops. When offered a command in a black outfit, some white officers flatly refused, forgoing promotion to a higher rank. Since West Pointers' choices of military post after graduation were based on class standing, it is significant that those cadets who ranked lowest in their class were most commonly assigned to serve with black soldiers.

Having been slaves or the children of slaves, black soldiers may indeed have initially had difficulty adjusting to army life, since they had few learned mechanical skills and for the most part were illiterate. The typical freed black man's dependence on others, learned in his early years under a brutal slavery, initially gave him less resourcefulness and initiative than was desirable for advancement through the military ranks.

Nevertheless, black soldiers excelled in discipline, morale, patience, and good humor in adversity, as well as demonstrating exceptional sobriety and physical endurance. In physique and physical condition, black soldiers were superior to most white men of the day, being usually about six feet in height and weighing two hundred pounds or more.[2] Their intelligence was considered equal to that of the regular army soldier, and, especially in the Twenty-fifth Infantry, their resistance to disease was notable. Only one man from the ranks of the Twenty-fifth Infantry was reported to have died from "climatic disease" while the troops were in Cuba, and only two died from any kind of disease at all.

Performance and talent usually were not enough, however, to overcome prejudice by civilian and military officials. Further evidence of the low esteem in which the black trooper was held by the high command is the rare instance in which a black received military honors, notwithstanding the actual reports of battlefield exploits and the reputation for courage black soldiers had among their fellow soldiers *and* their Indian enemies.

Indians, who had a deathly fear of black soldiers, called them "buffalo soldiers," reportedly because their hair resembled the hide of a buffalo. One white officer who had served with black troops for many years declared, "The most utterly reckless, daredevil savage . . . stands literally in awe of a Negro and the blacker the Negro the more he quails . . ." He added, "All four black regiments have been under fire in important Indian campaigns and there is yet to be recorded a single instance of a man in any of the outfits showing the white feather."

Another officer, certain that the Sioux would hand down to their childrens' children the story of a charge that two troops of black cavalry had made during the 1889 Pine Ridge troubles in South Dakota, described their way of fighting as follows: "It was at the height of the fracas and the bad Indians were regularly lined up for battle. These two black troops wanted to make the initial swoop upon them. They put up an incredible noise. Those two troops of blacks started their terrific whoop in unison when they were a mile away from the waiting Sioux, and they got warmed up and in better practice with every jump their horses made. I give you my solemn word that in the ears of us in the white outfits stationed three miles away the yelps these two Negro troops of cavalry gave sounded like the carnival whooping of ten thousand devils. The Sioux weren't scared a little bit by the approaching clouds of alkali dust, but, all the same, when the black troops were more than a quarter of a mile away, the Indians broke and ran as if the old boy himself were after them. It was then an easy matter to round them up and disarm them."

Because black soldiers performed so well in battle, even their severest critics (among them General William T. Sherman) attested to their steadfastness and bravery under fire.

All four black regiments of the U.S. Army were famous fighting units; yet the two cavalry commands had earned the most distinction. Moreover, the record of the Ninth Cavalry was unmatched during its thirty-two years of service in the Indian Wars. At that time, "the nigger ninth" was the most famous fighting regiment in the United States service. Many historians have commented on the effectiveness of the black soldiers in the Indian campaigns. The black soldier achieved a level of superior performance that reflected favorably not just on the black troopers, but on all members of the race, and ought to have proven to all who doubted their abilities and patriotism that Negroes were the equal of any American citizen.

Yet this record was for the most part officially unrecognized. At the time, the only decoration for personal bravery was the Medal of Honor, of which 416 were awarded during the Indian campaigns and Texas border conflicts of the 1870s. Although blacks accounted for about four thousand of the approximately thirty thousand soldiers involved in the warfare against the Indians, and participated in some of the fiercest fighting, only eighteen black cavalrymen received a Medal of Honor, with eleven of these going to members of the Ninth Cavalry. Not a single black infantryman was decorated during these years.

By the advent of the Spanish-American War, black regiments had an unusually large percentage of battle-tested veterans. In the years following the Civil War, a consistently high re-enlistment rate in black regiments and a correspondingly low 2 percent desertion rate were in striking contrast to an annual desertion rate among white troops of 30 or 35 percent.[3] This may have been because the black soldier looked on the military as a career, whereas the white soldier frequently sought out the army only as a temporary refuge. For blacks at the time, the Army may have been the only real career opportunity, however limited, in the white man's world. A large number of white officers of black troops also remained with the same outfit for many years. Possibly they were overlooked by the high command, or perhaps the authorities felt it would be too difficult to find a willing replacement. In any case, the overall result was intense unit pride, enhanced by increasing professionalism and superior performance, reinforced by a sincere desire among some black troops to show the world the potential of their race.

One can only imagine then what must have been the conflicting emotions of Sergeant Major Edward L. Baker toward his service in Cuba in 1898. Baker had been born in a freight wagon near North Platte River, Laramie County, Wyoming, on December 28, 1865, of pioneer parents, his father a Frenchman, his mother a mulatto. At age seventeen, Baker had joined the Ninth Cavalry Regiment as a trumpeter, serving five years fighting the Apaches in the Indian Border Wars. After those wars ended in 1887, Baker, who was fluent in Spanish and spoke some Russian; Chinese, and French, transferred to the Tenth Cavalry and advanced from private to sergeant-major.

An ambitious man, he applied in 1896 or 1897 for permission to attend the French Cavalry School at Saumur, France, offering to pay his own expenses. This request was enthusiastically endorsed by his superiors, but the Spanish-American War intervened. Baker went instead with the Tenth Cavalry to Cuba where he would distinguish himself in the Battle of San Juan Hill, earning a temporary commission as a second lieutenant and, in 1902, receiving the Medal of Honor for his heroic exploits. Only five Medals of Honor were issued to black troops during the entire Cuban War. Sergeant Major Baker was the only black soldier, in the cavalry or the infantry, to receive a Medal of Honor for bravery exhibited on the open field of battle.

In his later years, the highly intelligent Baker must have looked at his medal with some incredulity, knowing that regardless of his own valor, he was not alone among brave black soldiers. The black Twenty-fifth Infantry had never had a Medal of Honor recipient, although its troops had served valorously from the formation of their unit in 1869, throughout the Indian Wars (against both the Comanches and the Apaches), the war with Spain, and the battles of the Philippine Rebellion. Baker also knew that fighting on the southern slope of San Juan Hill alongside the black Twenty-fourth Infantry had been the white Seventeenth Infantry whose soldiers received nine Medals of Honor; whereas the troops of the Twenty-fourth received none. The Twenty-fourth had previously earned only two medals for bravery during twenty-nine years of Indian Wars, and these two had been awarded not for battlefield bravery but because two enlisted men had been instrumental in breaking up the celebrated Wham Payroll Robbery of May 11, 1889.

Of the eighteen Medals of Honor awarded to soldiers for bravery in the Spanish-American War, none was awarded to a black infantryman, even though these black soldiers had been in the forefront of the fighting, both at El Caney and at San Juan Hill.

If Sergeant Major Baker, rocking on his porch in retirement, wondered to himself about the striking contrast between the number of medals for bravery awarded black troops in the Spanish-American War in comparison to the number awarded white soldiers, what must he have remembered about his passage to Cuba in 1898 and the reception he and his fellows received on their return home?

The buffalo soldiers had served their careers in the West, at posts such as Missoula, Montana. There military officers had been a delightful addition to local society, according to a newspaper article published as the Twenty-fifth Infantry prepared in March 1898 to leave for Chickamauga, Georgia. The Missoula newspaper added that the black enlisted men had always comported themselves in a manner to win the respect of all citizens.

These cordial relations between white civilians and black troops did not thrive in the Deep South, however. The buffalo soldiers had experienced discrimination and disrespect even in the west, but they were not prepared for the outright hostility they were to face in Tennessee, Georgia, and Florida as they awaited passage to Cuba and their chance to die for their flag and nation.

Even the sea passage to Cuba was marked by rigid segregation. Some ships were segregated with blacks on one side and whites on the other, while other ships had a top-to-bottom segregation: blacks occupying the bottom decks and whites the top decks. Letters written by black soldiers after the hostilities state that, during the sea voyage, black troops were not allowed on deck except with special permission. When the *Concho,* one of the troop transports, finally reached the open sea, the brigade commander ordered that the two regiments on board, the black Twenty-fifth Infantry and the white Fourth Infantry, should not mix. This is ironic, because, having served together in Montana when the army had been used to restore order during labor union strife, the personnel of the two regiments were on the best of terms.

The white regiment was also allowed to make coffee first

each day, with a guard being detailed to be certain that this order was carried out. One soldier of the Twenty-fifth Infantry wrote that these restrictions were probably imposed to humiliate the blacks and noted that there was no word of protest from their officers.

In any case, the black troops reached Cuba and did their duty, as shall be shown. Then they returned to face what would be one of the most racist—and violent—eras of U.S. history.

Prejudice against blacks was so rampant immediately after the Spanish-American War that a group of black soldiers escorting a charge of Spanish prisoners from Tampa to Fort McPherson, Georgia, drew crowds wherever they stopped. The crowds showed more interest in taunting the black soldiers than in viewing the Spanish prisoners. In Huntsville, Alabama, that most valorous of the black regiments, the Tenth Cavalry, faced almost daily racial confrontations, which caused occasional bloodshed including the deaths of two cavalrymen. One black citizen of Huntsville was arrested for attempting to kill a soldier of the Tenth. On being questioned as to why he should be killing one of his own race, he replied that money was being offered for each black cavalryman killed.

Racial tensions among both blacks and whites were aggravated by the widespread newspaper publicity given to the almost daily racial incidents after black troops returned from Cuba. In a few cases, black soldiers resorted to force or threat to bring about the release of comrades thought to have been unfairly jailed, including one serious incident involving the Ninth Cavalry in Tampa, Florida.

Racial demagogues throughout the South thrived in such an atmosphere, so "Negrophobia" became even more rampant. Instances when black troops resisted discrimination and defied local racial customs conjured up dreadful prospects in the minds of white Southerners. This accelerated the collapse of what little remained of moderate white resistance to racism.

Added to the number of racial conflicts taking place in the States after the war were several incidents in Cuba involving "occupation forces" made up of black volunteer soldiers.

The presence of so large a contingent of black soldiers in Florida after the war and the problems related thereto probably hardened the attitudes of diehard racists among the white population, as well as causing questions to arise in the minds of moderates as to whether blacks could be assimilated in the culture of predominantly white America. As is true today, a majority of whites realized that the country was founded on the premise that all citizens are equal and every effort must be made to see that this ideal becomes a reality. Racial violence, unfortunately, is a complex issue. Some observers have felt that the heroism displayed by black soldiers in Cuba actually increased the resentment against them, especially among those white volunteers who had been left behind in Jacksonville, Miami, and other Florida cities.

It didn't help that some of the key players in the Spanish-American War allowed their initially positive assessment of black troops' performance to become tainted by racism. Roosevelt, who praised the "smoked Yankees" immediately after the war, recounted in *Scribner's* magazine several years later a tale that reflected on the courage of black soldiers. He stated that on the evening of the first day on San Juan Hill he had come upon two or three black soldiers who, having recently been in the battle on the summit, were descending the hill. Roosevelt pulled out his pistol and ordered them to return to the ranks of those who were still in the trenches. These men were under orders to head downhill to get food and water, since the troops on the hill had been fighting for many hours with no supplies of any kind. Roosevelt had misinterpreted the black soldiers' actions and was told of his mistake by officers nearby. On the following day he visited this black outfit and apologized for his mistake.

But Roosevelt made no mention of this in his later writings, except to say that on one occasion he had found it necessary to threaten some black soldiers with his pistol and turn them around because they were leaving the firing line. He maliciously added, despite overwhelming evidence to the contrary, that black soldiers were of little value unless led by white officers.

In his later years, Sergeant Major Baker no doubt weighed his service to his country against his country's treatment of himself and his fellow black soldiers and citizens. We have no way of knowing what he felt when he looked at his Medal of Honor. Nor can we know how he felt of the way history treated Teddy Roosevelt and the Rough Riders compared to the way it has treated the solders of the black units which campaigned in Cuba.

In any case, the period immediately after the Spanish-American War was a low point of U.S. race relations, perhaps reaching bottom during the administration of President Woodrow Wilson. The 1915 showing of a new motion picture, *The Birth of a Nation*, aside from being a breakthrough in movie-making technique, presented a hateful message and sparked race riots in at least five cities. The movie even inspired the reorganization of the Ku Klux Klan and was widely used as a recruiting tool for the hooded order.

Racial animosity became so widespread and was so deeply felt that any historian trying to recount events of the Cuban campaign would certainly have been influenced by the racial climate of the day. To indicate that black soldiers had actually been essential to the triumph over the Spanish army might even have made the historian subject to ridicule by both his peers and the general public. The history simply would not have been believed. Thus one can understand somewhat why the part played by black soldiers in this watershed event in American history has been largely overlooked by historians and, consequently, is generally unknown by the public.

1

Upon what meat doth this our Caesar feed, that he is grown so great?

—Shakespeare, *Julius Caesar*

America and Spain in the Late Nineteenth Century

By the last decade of the nineteenth century America had finally gained firm control of her western frontiers. Like a spirited youth who begins to realize there are new horizons to explore and untraveled worlds to conquer, America opened her eyes to the glimmer of opportunity on distant shores while, at the same time, threats by foreign nations were making American leaders increasingly conscious of her vulnerability.

The last three decades of the century were a period of transition for the United States; it changed from an agrarian country to one prospering from the remarkable benefits of the industrial revolution. American wealth and power were increasing each year. A quarter of a century after the great bloodletting of the Civil War the economies of the northern and eastern sectors of the nation were robust and expanding, whereas the hookworm-infested and pellagra-ridden South remained in the choking grip of post-Reconstruction politics, poverty, and increasingly violent racism.

Once freed from slavery, some blacks made rapid economic strides from 1865 to 1898. Overall, however, relations between the black and white races were not much improved. The conditions faced by blacks during this period were in many respects as brutal and dehumanizing as during slavery. In the period after the end of Reconstruction, racial prejudices took concrete shape in the laws of most Southern states as white-controlled legislatures codified statutes dealing with segregation, education, and voting.

My native city, Birmingham, Alabama, as racially divided as other areas of the South in the late 1800s, was in many other respects cut from different cloth. Using capital from the North, steel-related industries were founded and developed throughout the area known as Jones Valley, creating such a burst of wealth in the 1870s and 1880s that Birmingham soon came to be called the Magic City. The world's largest cast-iron statue, depicting Vulcan, the God of the Hearth, is still ensconced on a mountain top overlooking downtown Birmingham. Coal, iron, and steel had fueled the overnight growth of this "Yankee" city to a point where it was among the most prosperous in the nation, quite unlike most other Southern cities of the time.

Birmingham's prosperity mirrored America's new wealth, created by men of imagination and vigor, with industrial empires reaching into all sectors of the nation. Giant trusts such as John D. Rockefeller's Standard Oil, started in 1882, dominated more than 90 percent of the country's refining capacity. Lax laws relating to the formation of trusts, the transfer of stock ownership in corporations, and the formation of monopolies permitted those with adequate capital, sufficient determination, and a measure of ruthlessness to control the destiny of large segments of the American economy. Such industrialists as Andrew Carnegie, Henry Clay Frick, and J. P. Morgan dictated the prices of many key commodities, and when the United States Steel Company was formed by Morgan in 1903, it was capitalized at three times the annual revenue of the federal government.

As the nineteenth century closed, the industries of the United States were fast becoming the most productive in the world. Production of American steel had exceeded that of Great Britain in 1865, and by 1900, at ten million tons a year, it had surpassed that of Germany and Great Britain combined. As steel mills and factories pumped out their goods, dust coated everything nearby, and heavy pollution lay like a pall over the valleys, overshadowing the sun and obscuring visibility. Such was progress.

In both the South and the North, textile mills were processing more than 3.5 million bales of cotton a year. Large meat packing firms in the Midwest had turned to assembly-line production and were expanding rapidly.

Widespread prosperity had brought about a complacency toward foreign affairs, and despite the rapid growth in wealth, power, and influence of the United States government, Americans and their leaders were ill-prepared for the international responsibilities that would soon be thrust upon them.

Now, a century later, the United States, like Shakespeare's Caesar, "doth bestride the narrow world like a Colossus." With the twentieth century drawing to a close, the United States finds itself in a position of world influence and military strength unparalleled since the Roman Empire controlled all of Western Europe. It is staggering to imagine that this change has taken place over the span of a mere one hundred years—a century whose debut found the United States freshly victorious and fiercely optimistic following a short war with a significance that could not have then been anticipated.

Spain, too, was undergoing change. She had lost most of her American empire earlier in the nineteeth century when civil wars erupted throughout Central and South America. Colonial Spaniards had thrown off the imperial yoke, and the Spanish Empire never recovered. A progressive drop in national revenue over the ensuing years had seriously crippled the central Spanish government. More serious, perhaps, were the crippling economic effects of the failure to invest in agriculture, public works, and manufacturing—areas that other European countries were vigorously developing as the industrial revolution spread from England.

Spain's inability to reform long-standing abuses in her political structure had caused a gradual erosion of military capability over the course of the nineteenth century. The Spanish navy had become an archaic, expensive department of the government with a bulging shore-based bureaucracy. Rationed to twenty-four tons of poor-quality coal each day, battleships were unable to practice maneuvers, and, even worse, the Spanish fleet was allowed only one day of gunnery practice each year. It is not surprising that the fleet could not meet crises that involved traveling long distances and firing heavy weapons.

Meanwhile, the Philippines and Cuba were among the last strongholds of Imperial Spain. However, the Spaniards occupying Cuba were beset by a variety of troubles, and, from 1868 to 1878, an insurrection against Spanish rule had resulted in a hardening of attitudes on both sides.

The Cuban uprising was unlike earlier South American revolts. The latter, fomented by purebred Spanish settlers, had succeeded despite nominal participation by the natives and poorer classes. The Cuban insurrection of the late nineteenth century, on the other hand, had racial as well as economic overtones—in Cuba it was the freed slaves, their descendants, and the native inhabitants who attempted to cast off the colonial shackles.[4]

The Cuban economy was dominated by a handful of pure-blooded Spaniards who had strong ties with the motherland. These wealthy Spaniards controlled the western provinces of the island where the terrain was suitable for large-scale agricultural enterprises. They were planters. The native Cuban had a strong infusion of African blood and was so poor that, even in good economic times, his condition was only slightly better than that of a slave. These poverty-stricken Cubans occupied the eastern section of the island because it would support only small farms and could not produce agricultural wealth.

Hostilities between Spain and the Cuban rebels subsided after the signing of a peace treaty in February 1878. But the reforms introduced under the treaty were too little and too late. Separatist demands persisted, and open warfare between Cuban natives and the Spanish government broke out again in 1895.

Within a few years, thanks to the agitations of those in the United States who wanted to shake their nation out of its isolationist daze, that initial conflict would galvanize the attention of the American public and would develop into the Spanish-American War. In turn, that war would begin the U.S. ascent to the peak of world power.

2

There's a pinch of the madman in every great man.

—French Proverb

Impending War

Theodore Roosevelt was not just the best-known hero of the Spanish-American War. He was also significantly responsible for starting the conflict.

Isolationism—a strong leaning toward insularity and avoidance of foreign entanglements and international issues—was a potent political sentiment throughout the United States in the last decade of the nineteenth century. Shared at the time by many rich industrialists with powerful political connections, it was, however, a philosophy in opposition to the principles of such political leaders as Roosevelt and Henry Cabot Lodge. Roosevelt and Lodge believed that our young country, newly arrived on the world scene, was ready to strike out and secure a niche for itself in the international community more in keeping with its size, economic strength, and strategic location.

Addressing the isolationist sentiment, Roosevelt declared that Congress was "upholding, with pretended honor and mean intelligence, a national policy of peace with insult." Roosevelt believed that wealthy financiers and commercial interests cared nothing for national honor, especially if that honor conflicted even temporarily with business. Several newspaper chains of that time, heavily influenced by these industrialists and philanthropists, espoused isolationism; and slanted their reporting to discourage involvement with other nations' affairs.

The 1890s thus found the United States not only increasingly racist in its domestic attitude but also as xenophobic as it had been since the War of 1812 or the war with Mexico in 1848. We had, it seems, turned our focus inward in an effort to define who we were as a nation. Under the administrations of Benjamin Harrison (1889–1893), Grover Cleveland (1893–1897), and William McKinley (1897–1901), little was accomplished in the international arena, although momentous events were showing that other increasingly aggressive countries were willing to use military force to maintain and expand their empires. Events such as the Sino-Japanese War, the early signals of conflict in South Africa, the invasion of Ethiopia by Italy, and the acquisition of African states by most European countries did little to stir the United States from its complacency.

Following the carnage and the economic aftermath of the Civil War, the country and its political leadership had had their fill of things military. Economic forces heavily influenced the government, whose revenues were not only impaired by a slow economy but by the expenses related to Reconstruction in the South. Consequently, the military establishment rated a low priority when annual federal budgets were made, with this frugality continuing for the entire final third of the nineteenth century.

Federal revenues in the fiscal year 1889 were $225.8 million with expenditures low enough to yield a surplus of $57 million, and in 1892 federal revenues were $406 million, with a surplus of $52 million. In spite of the surplus revenues, Congress refused to authorize appropriations to modernize the army.

Plagued by diminishing operating funds, the army was faced with the challenge of pacifying the West by whatever means necessary to open it to migration and permanent settlement. To accomplish the final subjugation of the Indians, it was necessary for the army to spread its manpower far and wide throughout the West, first concentrating on the objective of controlling the Indians along the Mexican border and then doing battle with Plains Indians in the upper Midwest. The drying up of the military budget resulted in a progressive decrease in manpower. From a post-Civil War strength of fifty-six thousand men in 1867, the numbers gradually fell to twenty-five thousand enlisted men and two thousand officers in 1898. During the five years prior to the Spanish-American War, Congress had cut army manpower by half.

One could not, however, sidestep the reality of the international scene, where trouble was brewing in virtually every quarter. While many American policy makers had wisely come to the realization that military strength was essential to protect the growing economic interests of the United States, an isolationist-influenced Congress resisted all efforts at improving the nation's military capabilities.

In light of the dramatic changes taking place around the world, the United States did eventually see the wisdom of improving her military strength; but when the improvements came, they were unbalanced and poorly coordinated. American leaders showed foresight in upgrading the navy and bringing it up to standards equal to any nation in the world in speed and firepower. Yet, by the end of the 1890s, the United States Army remained seriously neglected and without appropriate funding. By any standard, it was dangerously undermanned and poorly equipped.

Singularly equipped by nature and by powerful political connections, Roosevelt was in a unique position to bring about the changes he thought desirable in America's foreign policy and military capacity. Possessing unlimited enthusiasm, great physical strength, and unsurpassed mental toughness, Roosevelt grew to be a formidable actor on the national scene.[5] There were many who shared his views of belligerent internationalism, but no one else was so strategically placed or sufficiently ambitious to turn aspirations into reality.

In many respects, Roosevelt resembled his peer across the Atlantic, the great German statesman Bismarck. Through a combination of determination, vision, and ruthlessness, Bismarck had pulled the German states into a coherent nation, which subsequently consolidated its power and influence by defeating Austria in 1866 and France in 1871. Both men had a political philosophy characterized by relentless and far-sighted diplomacy; both understood the essential connection between military power and statecraft; and both almost singlehandedly brought their nations to the brink of war.

Author at the age of twenty-three of what is still a definitive history of the American navy in the War of 1812, Roosevelt was as well informed as anyone in the country about the operations of the navy, its personnel and its equipment. He was especially concerned that the construction of technologically up-to-date battleships, cruisers, and naval vessels had become so complicated that it took two years to build any new vessel. Published in 1882, his book stated: "Since the change in military conditions in modern times, there has never been an instance in which a war between two nations has lasted more than two years. In the most recent wars the operations of the first ninety days have decided the result of the conflict."

Roosevelt felt it essential that Congress immediately authorize the building of more and larger ships whose mission could be offensive rather than defensive. Likewise, he expressed the need for better training and more modern weapons. Roosevelt's concern for updating and strengthening the navy spread to encompass the weak and unprepared army. He believed that the nation was dangerously weak militarily and thus in peril.

Reflecting his studies of naval history, his feelings were unequivocal: "[F]or the great English-speaking Republic to rely for defense upon a navy composed partly of antiquated hulks and partly of new vessels rather more worthless than the old" was simply a forfeiture of opportunities and a denial of responsibilities. Fortunately for the United States, Congress heeded Roosevelt and appropriated sufficient funds to create a Pacific fleet and a fleet in the Atlantic.

Also succumbing to Roosevelt's tireless exhortations, newly elected President William McKinley appointed the young firebrand assistant secretary of the navy in 1897. Roosevelt would use the position to influence governmental policy, an objective he vigorously pursued in a variety of ways, including direct conversations with President McKinley. His ideas exerted their greatest influence through the Naval War College, which, during the preceding decade, had evolved into the paramount source of war plans for the government.

On June 7, 1897, in the first great speech of his career, Roosevelt expressed to the Naval War College the need for military strength, repeating his opposition to those who did not have the same sentiments: "They wish the incompatible luxuries of an unbridled tongue and an unready hand." Nevertheless, he was encouraged that the navy had for years been gradually improving its ships and armaments. By 1897, the navy was in a much improved state of readiness for war, and even further enhancement took place during Roosevelt's one year as assistant secretary of the navy.

Roosevelt stated in his autobiography that as soon as he took over his new post he became even more convinced that war would come shortly. Roosevelt thought the situation in Cuba to be one of "murderous oppression" by Spain that would result in the complete devastation of an economy in which the United States had significant commercial interests related to its tobacco and sugar production. With Cuba's location near the proposed canal across Central America to the Pacific, the island was strategically situated, making it imperative that the country be in friendly hands.

To accomplish this Roosevelt felt it was essential for America to have adequate weapons with its most highly qualified men in the most critical positions.

The subordinate position of assistant secretary of the navy is usually not a platform for bringing about significant change in the navy or influencing government policy. However, Secretary of the Navy John S. Long, although a person of many virtues, was not equipped emotionally or physically to handle the job, preferring to take long vacations and to be at his office as little as possible. Roosevelt encouraged Long's propensity for rest, because it was during his many absences that Roosevelt moved up to acting secretary of the navy, a post from which he exerted great influence.

At his urging, the Navy Department, in June 1897, had published an updated war plan outlining in detail the exact strategic steps that would be taken if war with Spain became a reality. Included in the updated plan was a strategy for controlling the Philippines after defeat of the Spanish.

Within months, a visit to Havana by one of the ships of Roosevelt's navy would set off the spark that would put those war plans into effect.

3

Paradise is under the shadow of swords.

—Mahamet

War is Declared, April 1898

During times of peace, and even when some parts of the world are at war, protocol between nations has always allowed warships of a friendly nation to take up temporary station within the harbor of a friendly host. The visit is ostensibly to reinforce harmonious relations between two nations, but, for practical purposes, it helps immeasurably to ensure the safety of the visiting country's citizens in the host country. Sometimes such a visit is prolonged but creates no problem so long as both parties agree.

In late December 1897 and in January 1898, Cuba's capital, Havana, was wracked by disturbances set off by Spanish officers who targeted local newspapers for their reports disparaging Spain and her army. With their penchant for exaggerating events, American newspapers magnified the severity of the demonstrations, creating alarm in Washington. American diplomats contacted their Spanish counterparts and proposed a swap of visits by warships of each country. The agreement was that the American battleship USS *Maine* would visit Havana while the Spanish armored cruiser *Vizcaya* would make a call at New York. The Spanish agreed to the exchange, yet were surprised at the speedy American response. The *Maine* showed up the following morning, January 25, 1898, and dropped anchor in Havana harbor.

Thereafter, calm reigned in Havana and the Spanish officers, while cool toward American naval personnel, seemed to accept their presence without rancor. That the calm did not last was in part the fault of the popular press of the times, of which the most prestigious were the newspapers owned by the bitter adversaries William Randolph Hearst and Joseph Pulitzer. Each was determined to increase his newspaper's circulation at the other's expense as quickly as possible, using any means whatsoever, including publication of fabricated stories aimed at a gullible public. Before television, radio, or movie newsreels, newspapers were the only media. Hearst and Pulitzer exploited the newly developed technologies of printing and paper manufacturing which made newspapers a vehicle for the dissemination of news to the masses.

Each published articles detailing episodes of Spanish cruelty that had no basis in fact. The public mood quickly changed from neutrality to enthusiastic support of an American effort to teach Spain a lesson.

Although Spanish military forces in Cuba had been reinforced, hostile guerrillas controlled the countryside, and most Spaniards dared not show themselves except in cities. Some Americans, sympathetic with the cause of the oppressed rebels, smuggled weapons and ammunition into Cuba. While such assistance sustained the rebellion, it was insufficient to bring victory. It was enough, however, to weaken Spain, which had to supply substantial resources to combat the prolonged rebellion.

The heavy jungle of Cuba and the almost complete absence of roads made communication difficult for Spanish forces. Tropical diseases proved to be the most lethal foes of the Spanish army. In 1897, total Spanish army deaths in Cuba numbered 32,500, of which only five thousand were the result of military action. The balance of the deaths was due to yellow fever (eight thousand), malaria (seven thousand), typhoid fever, and diphtheria.

Cures for yellow fever and malaria were found only a few years after the Spanish-American War, thereby making possible the construction of the Panama Canal. Had the war been delayed by several years, the horrendous mortality from tropical disease and poor sanitation would have been avoided. From the early 1900s forward, military conflicts would no longer suffer morbidity from disease far exceeding that due to weapons and explosives. As ill luck would have it, however, in early 1898 the swelling tide of public opinion and events swept the unwilling combatants into a deadly embrace. War became inevitable.

The U.S. government had made it clear to the Spanish that the cruel repression of the Cubans was a cause for concern by Americans. The United States demanded autonomy for Cuban citizens and threatened intervention if this did not take place. In the early spring of 1898, in the absence of declared war but amid reports of ever-increasing Spanish brutality toward native Cubans, the United States began plans to send troops to Cuba to aid the insurgents. Among these troops, of course, were the black soldiers who are the focus of this study.

During the last years of the nineteenth century, a political faction known as the Carlists was expanding its influence in Spain. Don Carlos III, pretender to the Spanish throne, was a direct descendent of Charles X of France, which, in his opinion, made him the legitimate King of Spain. However, Alfonso XIII, a Hapsburg, was legal heir to the throne. Since he was too young to assume royal responsibility, Spain was under the rule of his mother, Maria Christina. As regent, Maria Christina was violently opposed to war with the United States; but she knew that failure to oppose the demands and accusations of the Americans could well lead to a Carlist uprising. Widespread civil war and loss of the throne would likely follow.

The Carlists, getting fresh hope from the troubles in Cuba, had raised a rebel army of some ten thousand soldiers in Spain and were said to have at least one hundred thousand supporters. Anything other than a declaration of war against the United States, or a modification of demands by the Americans, would have meant a revolution in Spain. Agonizing at America's increasing involvement in the Cuban conflict, Maria Christina sought the advice of her aunt, Queen Victoria of England. But Queen Victoria's ministers advised her not to lead a coalition of European sovereigns in an anti-American effort to request the United States to modify its demands on Spain.

With the exploitation of events by a virulent press, diplomatic relations between the two countries continued to worsen. Affairs reached a crisis in February 1898 when the contents of a letter from the Spanish ambassador to the United States became known to the American government. Addressed to a Cuban friend, the ambassador's letter disparaged several personal traits of President McKinley and criticized American newspapers. Extensive press coverage of the letter intensified the suspicions of many that the pro-war party in America (which now included both Hearst and Pulitzer) was trying to force a major crisis. The critical moment passed, however, and for a time tensions between the two countries slackened, allowing supplies of food to be sent from sympathizers in the United States to Cuba to aid the starving natives.

By February 15, 1898, the battleship *Maine*, resting at anchor for three weeks after its arrival in Cuba, had become more or less accepted as part of the scenery by those on shore. Early that evening, however, the ship suddenly exploded and sank, killing some 260 sailors. Despite several extensive investigations, no satisfactory explanation for the disaster has ever been forthcoming. Arguably the most thorough inquiry, by Admiral Hyman Rickover, which included all available evidence from Spain, suggests that the explosion was internal, possibly the result of error on the part of a sailor working with the ship's boilers.

In any case, the sinking of the *Maine* fanned the fires of jingoism in America. Events moved inexorably toward war. Aggravating the public's mood for war were the ever more realistic reports of Spanish brutality toward Cuban natives, some of whom were forced into deadly concentration camps. With events and details given constant full play in the press, it is not surprising that the president and Congress were increasingly influenced by the war fever gripping the nation.

Spain was rocked by its own war fever, and Maria Christina was finally impelled to declare war. President McKinley then sent his war message to Congress on April 11, 1898. Congress passed a joint resolution April 25 declaring war against Spain (retroactive to April 21) and proclaiming Cuba independent, empowering the president to take whatever steps were necessary to expel the Spanish from Cuba.

Showing political leadership at its weakest, both the United States and Spain had been driven to war by popular demand. The war would have profound consequences for each country, with one being stripped of the last remnants of its empire and the other acquiring unprecedented possessions and offshore commitments.

4

To win a war quickly takes long preparation.

—Latin Proverb

An Early Naval Success, May 1898

War was declared over the situation in Cuba, but the first battle of the Spanish-American conflict occurred halfway around the globe. It was the work of, not surprisingly, Theodore Roosevelt.

Roosevelt, always on the lookout for strong military commanders, had been impressed by the initiative and leadership shown by Commodore George Dewey a few years previously during a threatened altercation off the coast of Chile. Through political trickery, Roosevelt got President McKinley to appoint the aggressive Dewey as admiral of the navy's Asiatic fleet. Although a more senior officer, Commander John A. Howell, had been recommended for the post, Roosevelt outwitted Howell's supporters and arranged the appointment of Dewey as admiral of the Asiatic fleet. He accomplished this bit of chicanery by the simple expedient of first intercepting and holding a letter of recommendation for Howell, addressed to the president, and then persuading a friendly senator to urge McKinley to appoint Dewey to the post. When this unscrupulous strategy proved successful, Roosevelt had his aggressive fighter in command of the Asiatic Squadron.

In February 1898, anticipating an outbreak of hostilities, the navy telegraphed its squadrons to rendezvous at certain strategic points. After the sinking of the *Maine,* Roosevelt, as assistant secretary of the navy, and during one of the frequent absences of his superior, sent Dewey a cable instructing him to refuel in Hong Kong and then make certain that the Spanish fleet, waiting in Manila Bay in the Philipines, did not leave the Asiatic coast. Roosevelt's orders caused much consternation but were not countermanded by higher authority.

Dewey prepared for war. On May 1, 1898, he made a risky entry into Manila Bay, passing unscathed through the narrow mouth of the bay with Corregidor on one side and Bataan Peninsula on the other. The entrance to the bay was thought to be mined, but the adventuresome Dewey disregarded the danger. In fact, the entrance had been mined by the Spanish, but those who had sown the mines had merely thrown them in the water, where they had sunk eighty to a hundred feet to the bottom of the bay, harmless to any passing ships. Had the mines been properly placed, there is a good possibility that Dewey's fleet would have been turned back or at the least sustained significant damage.

However, once in the bay, Commodore Dewey's ships destroyed the entire Spanish fleet in a one-sided battle lasting only a few hours. Spain's wooden vessels were obsolete and their weapons were outmoded, although U.S. military intelligence was so poor that this came as a somewhat pleasant surprise.[6] Spanish gunners showed very poor marksmanship, and when one of their shells did hit its target it showed an extraordinary lack of killing power.

Unsubstantiated rumors that Dewey had wiped out the Spanish fleet soon reached the U.S., but no official confirmation could be given the American nation until the government had received a direct message from Hong Kong, where the telegraph office nearest to Manila was located. While the telephone, and especially the telegraph, were the technical means of communication over long distances, the actual messages transmitted could be easily intercepted. For this reason messages were sent in code, with the world's most secure and advanced code systems being in use by the United States Navy in 1898. The Bureau of Navigation of the Navy, in 1887, had printed the Navy Secret Code that was in use (except for a few changes) at the time of the Spanish-American War.[7]

A surface vessel traveled approximately seven hundred miles across the South China Sea from Manila to the Hong Kong overseas telegraph station in order to transmit news of the victory to the States, where the impatient Americans were in a fever of anxiety. Six days after the battle, on Saturday, May 7, 1898, Secretary of the Navy Long was handed the coded message.

Cryptographic officers of the Bureau of Navigation took the document to their offices and completed the decoding in about an hour. Not being one to avoid the limelight, Theodore Roosevelt had followed them to their offices and was the first high-ranking official to learn the contents of the message. Then, rather than turn the translation over to Secretary Long, he charged into a group of eager newspaper reporters and announced the victory and its details. Such callousness illustrates the temperament of Roosevelt, in that his ambitions drove him to ignore protocol, if by doing so he could further his public image and political career.

The news of Dewey's victory had yet to reach the United States, however, when a week after the declaration of war it was learned that a Spanish fleet had left Spain for Cuba with its purpose unknown. Deployment of the Spanish fleet, considered at the time to be formidable, confirmed the suspicions of those who felt that Spain was well-prepared for war and intent on holding its Caribbean colonies. Because of rumors about the Spanish fleet, the War Department cancelled a planned 5,000-man relief expedition to the Cuban coast. Instead, a flying squadron was sent from the United States fleet to protect the eastern coast of the United States from possible attack by the Spanish. Such extreme measures were taken on the flimsiest of information and decreased the concentration of American ships near Cuba. The Spanish admiral's mighty armada existed only in the imaginations of the Americans, since it consisted of but four armored cruisers, all only partially armed and no match for the American fleet. The Spanish fleet's destination was Santiago, Cuba, for maintenance and replenishment of coal supplies, of which there were little in Cuba.

American intelligence gathering resources were, by today's standards, quite primitive. But President McKinley was surprisingly successful in learning about Spanish plans, personnel, and troop and naval concentrations in Cuba, because the United States had a spy in the most sensitive part of the Spanish communication system. The spy, a Spaniard named Villaverde, served as a telegraph operator in the Governor General's palace in Havana. All incoming and outgoing telegrams, including those sent by the Spanish government, were sent from this office. The Spanish had established a censorship office to oversee all communications, but all offices were closed at night, allowing Villaverde to send his spy cables. Not only did he send out uncensored messages, but he read all incoming telegrams, including those relating to Spanish plans and troop and battleship dispositions.

Four telegraph cables stretched across the ocean floor of the Florida straits connecting Key West with Havana, and all cable traffic between Cuba and the United States was carried on these lines. Unbelievable as it may seem, by mutual consent of the governments of Spain and the United States, the Havana—Key West cable remained open. So well-kept was the secret of the Havana spy network that even Secretary of War Russell Alger seemed not to be aware of it, since he twice tried to have the Havana cable closed. He did not realize that nothing of real importance happened in Havana without President McKinley quickly knowing about it.

With Dewey's victory came enthusiasm for a more aggressive strategy in Washington. The navy asked the president to send army forces into Cuba to bolster a naval blockade. McKinley organized a meeting to consider launching an invasion of Cuba because he was encouraged by a report from General William R. Shafter (commander of the Fifth Army Corps at Tampa, who had previously been selected to direct the aborted expedition to run supplies to the rebels) that his fifteen thousand professional troops were ready and eager for action; with them he could quickly seize any point on the Cuban coast to serve as a base for operations. Havana had initially been selected as the target for the invasion force, but Army Commanding General Nelson A. Miles pointed out that Havana was the position of maximum Spanish strength. He then suggested a less heavily fortified site for the invasion, such as Santiago, the humid seaport on the southern coast of Cuba where the Spanish fleet was blockaded.

Santiago was chosen as the invasion objective, since capturing at least the fortresses at the mouth of its harbor might enable the American navy to destroy the Spanish fleet. Tampa was somewhat distant from Santiago in relation to other American coastal cities; however, since General Shafter's troops, including the black troops who had previously fought Indians in the West, were already assembled there, the high command selected the Florida city as the embarkation port for the invasion fleet.

Of all problems related to the command structure of the invading United States forces, possibly the most serious was lack of coordination between army and navy. Admiral Sampson, commanding the American fleet, expected the army to invade close enough to Santiago to reduce the batteries at the mouth of its harbor and thereby enable warships to enter the estuary and destroy the Spanish fleet. Shafter, whose plans were at complete variance with this, made no effort to inform the navy of his goals, which were to attack the hills surrounding Santiago, and, after enveloping the heights, to control the city. He hoped the Spanish fleet would then surrender or move out into the open sea and try to escape the American fleet. Shafter was prescient in one respect: he felt it urgent that the campaign be very rapid and rushed to a quick conclusion, since he was obsessed by fear that the tropical climate of Cuba could cause such widespread disease among his army that it would become entirely disabled.

In spite of the United States' extensive military preparations that included the mobilization of troops, the procurement of large quantities of supplies, the renovation of cargo ships into troop ships and the many other details related to an overseas invasion, General Shafter was correct in that the principal threat to success of the invasion continued to be the likelihood of disease among the troops. Not endemic malaria, but severe and often fatal gastrointestinal diseases resulting from poor sanitation and inadequate equipment posed the greatest threat to life. Additionally, the recent onset of a yellow fever epidemic in Cuba had caused an increasing number of deaths among both the native population and the Spanish troops and was to prove even more calamitous for the American forces.

5

It takes a very little yeast to leaven a lump of dough . . . it takes a very few veterans to leaven a division of doughboys.

—General George S. Patton

Of Veterans and Volunteers

Of all wars in which the United States has participated, the Spanish-American War is the only one fought and won almost exclusively by military career professionals, including a large number of black veterans of the Indian Wars in the West.

In the Spanish-American War the regular soldiers and officers of the army and navy were substantially the sole participants in military action. The military high command had intended from the outset to recruit relatively small numbers of volunteers, who were to be trained and equipped with the limited resources available for that purpose. However, public enthusiasm for the war, especially within the National Guards of each state, applied political pressures on Congress. As a result, a vigorous recruitment campaign was funded, resulting in a huge outpouring of volunteers whose number eventually reached two hundred thousand men by the first month of the war. The only draft necessary for the Spanish-American War was provided by the winds of strident publicity. Virtually all of the volunteers, however, sat out the war in various miserable camps on the eastern seaboard and in Florida.[8]

Of the few volunteer soldiers actively involved in the fighting in Cuba, only the First U. S. Volunteer Cavalry brought honor to themselves as a unit for discipline and heroism on the field of battle. Rather than remain a subordinate under the secretary of the navy, Theodore Roosevelt, eager to experience actual combat, had persuaded the army to make him a colonel in a volunteer cavalry unit. Roosevelt's nationwide popularity had been such that news of his assembling a regiment for military duty against Spain resulted in an impressive number of volunteers, a total so great that he was able to select only one in twenty. Roosevelt, with no experience in warfare, wisely chose not to request the position of commanding officer; instead, he recommended as leader of the volunteer cavalry troops Colonel Leonard Wood, a regular army medical officer with considerable leadership experience in fighting Indians. So widespread was its fame that the First Volunteer Cavalry attracted nicknames including "Teddy's Terrors," "Teddy's Texas Tarantulas," and "Teddy's Gilded Gang," but Roosevelt let it be known that none of the sobriquets was suitable. Eventually the group was referred to as "Roosevelt's Rough Riders," a name which stuck.

Of course, the largest part of the credit for the eventual success of the Rough Riders should go to their veteran leaders, Colonel Wood and General Joseph Wheeler, seasoned warriors who had led troops under fire in previous wars. This is not to detract from that novice officer, Theodore Roosevelt, who, in spite of no formal training in military leadership or tactics, had fighting instincts and martial spirit the equal of any professional officer.

Only two other volunteer regiments participated in the invasion. Unfortunately, one of these volunteer regiments broke under fire and did little to contribute to the strength of the attack on San Juan Hill, while the other was withdrawn from the battle on the hillside at El Caney because smoke from outmoded rifles disclosed the troops' position and attracted an inordinate amount of enemy fire.

Consequently, it was regular Army troops who shouldered the burden of attacking the well-entrenched Spanish Army, and among these regular troops were the four black regiments, the Ninth Cavalry and Tenth Cavalry, and the Twenty-fourth Infantry and Twenty-fifth Infantry.

When it authorized the raising of a volunteer army, Congress also directed the recruitment of ten thousand enlisted men "possessing immunity from diseases incident to tropical climates." Without explicitly saying so, the military decided to use black soldiers in the tropics based partly on evidence of the seeming natural resistance of northern African natives to tropical diseases, an empirical conclusion the Spanish had reached after centuries of maintaining possessions in the tropical areas of the Western Hemisphere. Another expression for black soldiers was "the Immunes."[9]

As has been mentioned earlier, the black troops were seasoned veterans and would play a significant role in the fighting to come. Their effectiveness was further increased by remarkable regimental pride and unity. And as will be seen, they also played a major and heroic role in battling the disease that gripped the U.S. troops after the Spanish were beaten.

Most pressing among the problems of the United States army at the time was a defective command structure. A cumbersome apparatus existed through the years of the Indian conflicts causing countless inefficiencies and much frustration on the part of many high ranking officers. The disarray evolved from the unnatural division of the army command into two separate segments: line officers and field officers. Line officers lived in Washington where they exerted their influence, while the less influential field officers remained distant from the sources of power. Having usurped all command and planning activities within the army, line officers had developed inappropriate power and each had developed his own small kingdom with its own bureaucratic infrastructure. Naturally, line officers resisted any change in such a system, for their positions and prestige allowed them to plan campaign strategies and military operations with very little input from field officers.

In this country there has always been conflict over who should wield the reins of power, the states or the federal government. The tension between these two competing forces is inherent in our system of government and the battle heats up only when one side gains too much power. Local autonomy arguably does make for a more efficient and enthusiastic operation of government, and the division of responsibilities between field officers and line officers is not much different. Naturally, the military must create long range strategy and be able to exercise control over the game plan, but this control must be tempered by the exigencies in the field and should not stymie decision making by field officers.

At the time of the Spanish-American War, line officers frequently exerted their influence through subordinate officers in the field, bypassing even commanding generals if they so desired; so field commanders were often left on the sidelines when important decisions were being made. Throughout the period of preparations for the war, line officers in Washington decided what equipment, weapons and supplies would be needed. The commanding officer of the invasion forces, General William R. Shafter, had little to say as to whether or not supplies were suitable for the task at hand. Thus General Shafter was, in this respect, reduced to a figurehead, required to carry out the strategy of higher-ups with no voice in selection of tools to do his job. In spite of this, he knew he would be held accountable for the results of the campaign.

Adding to the difficulties of the U.S. Army was the fact that fiscal control over all military expenditures was in the hands of the secretary of war, leaving the commanding general of the army, Nelson A. Miles, in control of military discipline, training, and planning.[10] But, without the approval of the secretary of war, he had no freedom to dispense the funds he thought necessary to accomplish his goals. Ultimately, Elihu Root, secretary of war under both McKinley and Roosevelt, brought about fundamental changes in army organization. In the first decade of this century, modifications that Root implemented finally gave field officers more responsibility and accountability for the troops under their command.

With war fast approaching in March of 1898, the initial absence of forceful direction from above posed a serious problem for the army, since it did not know whether a large or small campaign was in the offing. At that time McKinley had not formulated any concrete plans regarding an ultimate objective or how it was to be reached. Six weeks before the declaration of war, Congress appropriated fifty million dollars for national defense, but McKinley had interpreted "defense" in its literal sense and had permitted the funds to be used only for coastal defenses. Until more leadership was shown by a seemingly laggard president, not even tentative plans could be made.

Said to be easily influenced by whomever he had last talked to, McKinley had the demeanor of a great leader but was actually a somewhat indecisive commander. When he did finally communicate his goals, war had already been declared. He had shown enough initiative, however, to set up a command post in the White House that allowed coordination of the top brass of the army and navy with his personal advisors. A unique feature of this War Office was the array of twenty-five telegraph wires connected to various cities and military departments in other cities. Fifteen special telephones completed an electronic communication network that was the first such command center ever available to a commander-in-chief.

In spite of his proclivity for long weekends, Secretary of the Navy Long had proven to be a very satisfactory administrator with extremely capable subordinates, such as Roosevelt and

Admiral Dewey. McKinley turned preparations for naval warfare over to them. Because of commendable foresight in developing a Navy War Board ten years previously, the Navy Department dominated the development of military strategy. The board was of great assistance to the president in developing his plans, but, as would be expected, the navy was for a time accused of taking over the planning for the war. In early 1898, the army developed a similar board that was made part of a joint board for direction of the war. However, in April 1898, President McKinley intervened in army affairs because of what seemed to him increasing evidence of the poor judgment and poor management of Secretary of the Army Russell A. Alger. McKinley had gradually come to doubt Alger's ability to run his department efficiently.

President McKinley also had developed an increasing distrust of General Miles, who had been appointed commanding general of the army by President Cleveland solely on the basis of his seniority, and he could not be fired or transferred until the age of retirement. General Miles was experienced in fighting small campaigns against the Indians, but he had little knowledge of how to manage large armies. Coupled with a strong athletic physique was a brusqueness of manner and tactless nature that made him an imposing and forbidding leader, paricularly when combined with his imperious countenance set off by a large iron-grey mustache. Miles had little respect for those civilians who considered themselves authorities on things military and evidently did little to hide this feeling. Not only did he quickly alienate Secretary Alger, but he also fell from the graces of the president, whose confidence he had at first enjoyed.

Alger had served as a general in the Civil War and had later made his fortune in the timber business, but his overweening egotism and hypersensitivity made it difficult for him to effectively manage a department in which there were already many strong-minded aggressive individuals. His elegant profile, accentuated by a carefully trimmed goatee, gave him the appearance of an academician, while his vanity and impulsiveness made him difficult to work with as he labored to establish control over the complexities of the Army organization.

In the Spanish-American War both General Miles and Secretary of the Army Alger lacked the traits of character to enable them to be effective. Alger was incapable of reining in General Miles. Miles alienated his superiors, therefore, his excellent and well-considered military advice to defer the invasion of Cuba until after the rainy season ended in October was completely ignored.

6

A man who is good enough to shed his blood for the country is good enough to be given a square deal afterwards. More than that no man is entitled to, and less than that no man shall have.

—President Theodore Roosevelt

Invasion Preparations

March in Montana is often a wintry month; cold blasts from Canada, accompanied by driving snowflakes, give little portent of what is to come. But, even so, nature is always on the verge of breaking from the chill grip of old winter, preparing to throw herself into the youthful arms of spring.

During the last days of March 1898, a brief warm spell had thawed the countryside. At Ft. Assiniboine, Montana, Companies C and E of the black Twenty-fifth Infantry regiment, under the command of Captain Walter S. Scott, were stationed with units of the black Tenth Cavalry. Because of the unusually pleasant early spring the company had been able to drill frequently and continue the combat training that had been in progress for some five or six years.

Such training had been diligently pursued under the direction of the regimental commander, Colonel Burt, and was to prove invaluable in Cuba. Previously, very little formal combat training had been given to troops in the West, because Indian fighting did not follow the techniques prescribed in traditional army manuals. Since June 1880, some eighteen years before, companies of the Twenty-fifth Infantry had not served together as a unit because they had been widely distributed throughout the northern plains. Army authorities had dispersed companies throughout the West because of a chronic shortage of military manpower; so it was rare that more than three or four of any regiment's companies ever were together at the same place.

At Ft. Missoula, Montana, late one day in March 1898, the chaplain of the Twenty-fifth Infantry, T. G. Steward, noticed the trumpeter of the guard hurry out of the adjutant's office with a dispatch in his hands and run briskly toward the quarters of the commanding officer. Within a few minutes there was an officers' call, so all officers of the post hastened to the Administration Building to learn the news. The commanding officer demanded how much time each company commander would need to prepare his unit for transfer to a permanent station elsewhere, and how long each would require to arrange for settlement of his family. The colonel agreed to allow them ten days for all preparations to be made.

With war-clouds gathering, everyone thought the Twenty-fifth Infantry would be sent to the Dry Tortugas, off Key West, Florida, and from there would go to Cuba. However, orders directed the men of the Twenty-fifth Infantry to store their furniture in a large gymnasium at the post and prepare to travel to Chickamauga Park, Georgia, a short distance from Chattanooga,

Tennessee. Similar orders instructed all separated companies of the regiment to board trains and meet the regiment in St. Paul, Minnesota, from where they would travel as a unit to Chickamauga.

Troops of the Twenty-fifth Infantry had endeared themselves to the people of Missoula, where they had been stationed for many years under the command of the gentlemanly Colonel Burt. Upon receiving the news of the Twenty-fifth's imminent departure, the affection felt by the community for the black troops surfaced in a long article in the *Daily Missoulian*. It stated that the officers and ladies of the post would be missed since they had been a delightful addition to local society and that strong friendships formed between officers and townspeople would suffer when severed.

The article further noted that the black enlisted men of the regiment had always comported themselves in a manner to win the respect of all citizens. The newspaper anticipated a problem that would cause much suffering for the troops: they would abandon the lovely climate of Missoula for the sultry weather of the tropics. Warm sentiments were expressed: "Colonel Burt is such an officer that he could lead his soldiers into the jaws of hell if he were ordered to do so. If there be war, the fortunes of the Twenty-fifth Infantry will be followed with interest by the public of Missoula, who are satisfied that, though it is a dark regiment, not a white feather will be shown."

Since the Twenty-fifth Infantry was the first regiment to mobilize for war, its progress from Montana to Chickamauga created nationwide interest, attracting daily attention of newspapers and the illustrated press. Such was the publicity that enthusiastic crowds, acting as though fighting had already begun, greeted them at every station. A crowd gathered at the Union Depot Station of St. Paul, Minnesota, to meet the black troops and to decorate the train engine with flags in their honor. Black soldiers noticed, however, that as the train moved deeper into the South toward Georgia the crowds grew smaller with each new railway station.

Fort Chickamauga had been the site of a crucial Civil War battle in which several officers of the regiment had fought. Since he was the first regimental commander to set up camp at the park, Colonel Burt had the privilege of naming the camp in honor of a friend, General Boynton, alongside whom he had fought for the Union on the Chickamauga battlefield.

Most of the regiment's companies assembled in Georgia within weeks of receiving their original orders. Two companies never arrived, however, since they had been sent to Key West, Florida, only to be sent back to rejoin the regiment at Tampa, Florida, later in May.[11] The extra travel was caused by poor planning and poor judgment on the part of the high command, because at Key West fresh water was available in only small quantities from a few dug wells. The price of fresh drinking water multiplied ten times during the few days the troops remained there.

Black troops, seeing the South for the first time in many years, met with unfamiliar challenges related to being stationed in the southern part of the United States. While in the West, they had encountered segregation and discrimination on many occasions, so they were familiar with its nastiness, but they had very little comprehension of the ferocity of true Southern Jim Crow segregation.[12] Black troops were shocked when, on entering Chattanooga, local proprietors denied them service at restaurants and shops within the city. In Western towns citizens had at times refused service to blacks garrisoned nearby and had even heaped abuse upon them, though the soldiers were usually the town's only defense against hostile Indians. This was the exception, however, not the rule.

But black troops had never before been stationed in the eastern part of the United States where racial hostility reigned supreme; in fact, it had been the practice of the United States Army not to station black troops east of the Mississippi River, because their acceptance by white communities was doubtful. In the early years of the decade a company of the black Tenth Cavalry had been stationed at a camp in Virginia but was quickly moved west of the Mississippi because of the outcry from local citizens.

Because it was in Georgia, Chickamauga Park proved to be an unfortunate choice for assembly of black troops from the West. The Georgia legislature had been the first state legislature to pass a Jim Crow law authorizing streetcar conductors to separate the races "as far as possible." Consequently, black troops traveling on street cars into Chattanooga were made to occupy segregated seats. Increasing racial tension developed in Chattanooga because of mistreatment of black troops, who had such self-esteem and *esprit de corps* that they refused to be segregated or denied services that they considered their right.

Feelings ran so high that regimental officers took from the troops all sidearms to prevent violent reprisals in response to the demeaning segregation practices that blacks ran into at every turn. Because of the indignity of having to ride from Chickamauga to Chattanooga in Jim Crow cars, The Twenty-fifth Infantry troopers pledged not to ride again on segregated public transportation "unless ordered to by official command." They elected to walk or hire private transport.

Black infantry units stayed at Chickamauga Park for less than a month before moving to Tampa in early May. During the month all regiments were brought up to wartime strength by the addition of enough volunteers to fill gaps in the ranks, and a few new regiments were formed using twenty-five or thirty veteran regulars as a core group. On May 7, 1898, with companies arriving in Tampa from three separate stations, the Twenty-fifth Infantry Regiment finally assembled as a unified regiment for the first time in eighteen years. To their sorrow, they learned that their much beloved Colonel Burt had been promoted and reassigned.

Upon hearing the news late one afternoon, the men of the regiment spontaneously gathered in front of the colonel's tent calling out to him that they did not want him to leave. Many of them, kneeling on the ground, prayed for his safekeeping and quick return. The soul-stirring demonstration took place at dusk and caused some officers of long service to remark that they had never seen anything similar to such a demonstration of affection for an officer.

The black Twenty-fifth Infantry Regiment joined the First

and Fourth Infantries to form the Second Brigade of the Second Division of the Fifth Army Corps. Colonel Evin Miles, who replaced Colonel Burt, was well acquainted with its officers and troops because he had served with the regiment during the Indian Wars. He chose Lt. Colonel Aaron S. Daggett to be his subordinate commander. During their stay in Tampa, all regiments drilled rigorously in combat exercises in preparation for the work ahead. Such drills were not only for instruction of the new volunteers but were an attempt to acclimate all men to the unaccustomed rigors of a subtropical climate. So intense was the Florida heat, aggravated by the wearing of woolen uniforms, that drill hours were limited to early mornings and dusk.

Tampa had some eighteen thousand men (of whom four thousand were black) and twenty thousand horses and mules squeezed into its limited space, so some troops were sent to nearby Lakeland, Florida, where a total of twenty thousand were finally stationed. In Lakeland, police arrested two soldiers of the black Tenth Cavalry for shooting a white man in a brawl related to a barber's refusal to give one of the black soldiers a haircut. The *Tampa Morning Tribune* of June 14 stated that at the soldiers' trial a jury convicted one soldier of murder while the other was acquitted for lack of evidence.

A developing tourist city with a population of just twenty-six thousand, Tampa had only one major hotel, the Tampa Bay Hotel, built by millionaire entrepreneur H. B. Plant. Plant was also owner of a large railroad in Florida that stood to profit mightily from the transport of troops and supplies related to the war. The elegant hotel, temporary residence of many high-ranking officers, served also as headquarters for the large horde of newspaper reporters that descended on the city. Theodore Roosevelt spent three nights at the hotel with his wife, who was convalescing from a brush with death from a long, undiagnosed abdominal abscess. Featuring a very wide veranda and a large number of luxurious rooms, the Tampa Bay Hotel was so comfortable that some newspaper reporters called this period of the conflict "the Rocking Chair War." Approximately one hundred eager war correspondents, representing all major newspapers and all the leading magazines in the country, had swooped into the city to be on hand for their "Newspaper War."

Meanwhile, racial tensions mounted continuously between black troops and the white citizens of Tampa, as well as between veteran black troops and white soldiers, most of whom were volunteers. On June 6, the night before assembling for embarkation, a serious disturbance flared up when a drunken white soldier grabbed a black child from its mother and entertained his comrades by holding the child head-down and spanking it with one hand. To prove their marksmanship, several white soldiers started shooting in the direction of the child. One shot went through the sleeve of the boy's shirt; however, the child was not injured and was returned to its distraught mother.

Fresh from duty in the West, a contingent of black soldiers of the Twenty-fourth and Twenty-fifth Infantry Regiments accosted the drunken white troops because they viewed the behavior of the white Ohio volunteers as anything but sporting. A rampage exploded, in which black soldiers stormed into the saloons and cafes that had refused to serve them. They even forced their way into the white brothels where, as the *Morning Tribune* disdainfully reported, "white and black inmates were forced, at the point of pistols, to submit to the men who were disgracing the uniform of the United States."

The fighting spread to involve not only white soldiers but a number of white residents as well. Called out to quell the disturbance, the Provost Guard and the Tampa police were overwhelmed by the violence of the rampage; so the authorities called troops from the Second Georgia Volunteer Infantry, a white regiment, to restore order. Undoubtedly, the white Georgia boys had much satisfaction in quelling the riot. To their credit, they accomplished this with no loss of life, although there were many wounded. Evidence of the extent of the violence is that twenty-seven black troops and a number of white soldiers were sent to the hospital at Fort McPherson, near Atlanta, for treatment of their wounds.

The *Atlanta Constitution* editorialized that the Tampa disturbance "clearly proved that army discipline has no effect on the Negro." Other newspapers cavalierly pointed out that the black soldiers had even outraged white prostitutes though "these women were of the lowest type." The first newspaper publication reporting details of the riot noted that: "the streets ran red with blood," but only sketchy reports were available thereafter because of strict military censorship.

Given the intolerable climatic conditions of persistent heat and high humidity, it is not surprising that the troops, clothed in heavy woolen uniforms, finally reached a boiling point as the result of so much unmistakable social hostility. The tolerance and restraint of the black troops had worn thin. Whatever actually happened to unleash the fury of the black regulars, reports of the disturbance and the widespread publicity resulting from it seriously affected the public's attitude about the stability and quality of black personnel in the army.

Evidently the military authorities decided not to investigate the cause of the Tampa riot and chose not to mete out justice for instigating the riot. In calmer times such anarchic behavior would have most certainly brought forth swift retribution, but on the day after the riot all troops were ordered to board troop ships in preparation for the voyage to Cuba. Before assembling his troops for embarkation, one white officer of the black Tenth Cavalry tried to arrange for his men to eat in local restaurants but was refused service. The typical response to his inquiries was voiced by a lady proprietor who stated: "to have colored men eat in my dining room would ruin my business."

The venting of so much prejudice against blacks caused black chaplains and other black leaders throughout the country to speak out, commenting that these black soldiers were going to Cuba to free a largely black population from Spanish domination. Their feeling was that it was hypocrisy to think that they were going to be doing any good, since black citizens of the United States suffered from a repression similar to that in Cuba. To them there seemed little difference between Spanish brutality to the black Cuban and American brutality to the American black. One could be led to believe in the face of such hypocrisy that the widely publicized American concern for the downtrodden native Cubans was actually no more than a pretext for an economically motivated, aggressive interventionist foreign policy that had nothing to do with fine principals espoused by the American constitution.

Local white Tampa residents had not been the only group involved in severe racial disturbances with black troops. Using vigorous recruitment efforts, the army had enrolled a large number of whites from many different parts of the country. These soldiers naturally brought with them the racial attitudes of their diverse regions, which were little different from those in the South. Racial prejudice was widespread throughout the United States and racial tensions surfaced whenever whites and blacks were thrown together in the army. The violent racial confrontation occurring in Tampa showed this to be the case.

Although Tampa was located some four hundred nautical miles from Havana and much farther from other Cuban objectives, the high command gave little consideration to any other embarkation point. They were convinced the Tampa facilities were adequate to support the loading of a large military force, a miscalculation which proved to have distressing consequences.

In the nineteenth century America had gone to war many times, but this was only the third occasion in which armed forces of the United States had made preparations for embarkation of a contingent of soldiers for action away from the continent. Except for a small naval group of marines and sailors deployed in May 1803 on the shores of Tripoli to burn Moorish felucas and another contingent of troops landing in eastern Mexico in 1847 during the Mexican War, Americans had never undertaken an invasion from the sea.

In view of such inexperience, it is not surprising that many problems developed in the planning and implementation of the expedition. Primary among the problems was the expectation that the army supply services would clothe and equip about forty thousand troops. Political pressures had caused the government to call up five times that number of volunteers, over two hundred thousand troops in all, far exceeding the resources available to care for them. As a consequence, the volunteers were stationed in various camps along the east coast, with the majority in Florida.

Utter confusion developed when supplies, sent by railroad from over the country to support the invasion forces, were stored in boxcars without labels or invoices. During the later fighting in Cuba, the haphazard manner in which supplies had been loaded and labeled on the transports caused very serious shortages of rifles, ammunition, clothing, medical supplies and food. An officer looking for beans might open a container to find leather shoes.

Boxcars containing vital provisions of many varieties remained on railroad sidings, with no one knowing what was inside, and the congestion of freight cars on the railroad extended for some twenty miles outside of Tampa. Troops and supplies moved very slowly over a single-line railroad that served the embarkation dock. Wagons and 2,295 mules or horses were placed in the bottoms of the ships, where conditions were so bad that some of the livestock died before the ships had even left the dock. Although thirty-three vessels were available to carry the expeditionary forces, there was room at the dock for only eight at a time, and the congestion in the harbor from ships trying to find a place at the dock became so great that two troop ships collided.

Pity the poor soldier wearing woolen clothing in the sub-tropical heat of June in Florida. Because the Army had never made plans for operations in the subtropical or tropical regions, the common soldier had to wear a woolen uniform. While woolen clothes are perfectly satisfactory for wear in the upper western states, they were to prove a cause of much discomfort and suffering for that unfortunate man required to wear them in the tropics. Since lightweight clothes were not available, the heat of both Florida and Cuba caused much distress, a miserable situation made worse by the short time available to become acclimated to the torrid, humid tropics.

Theodore Roosevelt's troops had no such problems, how-ever. The Rough Riders, as these troops came to be known, were comprised of actors, New York policemen, doctors, frontier sheriffs, prospectors, a score of Indians, society leaders, profes-sional gamblers and an unknown number of renegades and escaped convicts who had assumed other identities for the occa-sion. Along with men named Wadsworth and Tiffany were famous college athletes, the world's greatest polo player, a legend-ary Harvard quarterback, the United States tennis champion, track stars from Yale, and Hamilton Fish, Jr., who had captained the Columbia crew. Included in this curious mélange were fifty young men from the best colleges and clubs in the East, all superb athletes, with horsemanship being all that the motley assortment had in common.

When the Rough Riders initially assembled they had worn their own clothes, but, by the time they had reached Cuba, most of them were dressed in the new regulation uniform of khaki breeches and blouses with blue flannel shirts. Supplied with hastily requisitioned lightweight pants and shirts, the Rough Riders became the only outfit in the entire army that was appropriately clothed for tropical weather. To facilitate procurement of necessary clothing and supplies for his troops, Theodore Roosevelt had remained in Washington for a time before joining his regiment.

By using his influence with the secretary of the army, he had been able to cut red tape and clothe his troops in the new light weight khaki uniforms. (Roosevelt himself was clothed in a uniform tailored by Brooks Brothers of New York.) On June 9, 1898, a brief note appeared in the *New York Times* stating that the War Department had at last found a material suitable for uniforms worn in the tropics, and that the army had signed a few contracts for production of these uniforms. The Army sent some five thousand heavier-weight canvas khaki uniforms to Tampa to replace the woolen uniforms of the regular army soldiers, but these proved to be just as hot as the woolen clothing and did not have the same durability.

Because of the known shortage of modern Krag-Jorgensen rifles, Roosevelt was fearful that his troops would be issued the obsolete Springfield rifle. Thanks to the influence of Colonel Wood, the Rough Riders received the regular cavalry carbines rather than the black-powder Springfields issued to all other volunteer outfits. The issuance of these weapons to his volunteer troops pleased Roosevelt immensely, since he assumed (correctly, it turned out) that those troops equipped with the better rifles of the regular cavalry would go immediately to the front for fighting.

Primarily because its colorful Lieutenant Colonel Theodore Roosevelt had political aspirations and a penchant for publicity, the Rough Riders would win more newspaper attention in Cuba that all other units combined. General John J. Pershing, the World War I hero who served in the Spanish-American War as quartermaster officer of the black Tenth Cavalry, commented in his autobiography on the war record of Theodore Roosevelt and the political benefits he reaped from it: "It is safe to say that in the history of the country no man ever got so much reward for so little service." Pershing added further: "It was the extensive publicity he received rather than the actual service that brought him such exceptional political preferment."

Roosevelt stated in his memoirs that, by the time the First Volunteer Cavalry had reached Tampa, they were better equipped than most of the regular regiments (and far better than the other two volunteer units that were part of the invasion forces). Moreover, when Roosevelt heard it would be thirty days before he could get horses for his troops, he pulled strings as before and was issued horses immediately, a futile effort since all requisitioned cavalry horses, except those for the highest-ranking officers, were left behind—the cavalry, it was learned, would fight as dismounted troops in Cuba.

7

How similar is an ocean voyage to the voyage of death, the voyage of
eternal life!

—Juan Ramon Jiménez, *Nocturno Sonado*

Into the Unknown

Early in June 1898, Admiral Sampson's fleet blockading
Santiago harbor bombarded both the forts at the mouth of the
harbor and the city itself, inflicting some damage to the Spanish
fleet within the harbor. He imparted a sense of urgency in his
dispatch to the Navy Department in Washington, stating that he
had bombarded the forts at Santiago from a distance of two
thousand yards and felt that a force of ten thousand seasoned
regulars could take the city and fleet within forty-eight hours. He
urged that an assault on the city not be long delayed because the
city would soon be defended more strongly by guns taken from
the fleet.[13]

The high command had anticipated Sampson's urgent message by ordering troops on June 6 to strike tents and be ready to
move to the dock at Port Tampa, situated on the bay several miles
from the city, in preparation for embarkation. Transportation to
move their baggage did not appear until the next morning, when,

after several more hours of waiting, they finally left for the railroad station to Port Tampa.

On the subject of shipping and transportation of troops and supplies, the always practical yet poetic Winston Churchill once wrote: "Victory is the beautiful, bright-colored flower. Transport is the stem without which it never could have blossomed." Before embarking, General Shafter, in command of the invasion forces, realized that the available transports could not accommodate his entire corps. Realizing that the twenty-five thousand troops stationed in Tampa (out of the two hundred thousand troops available in reserve) would not fit into thirty-two transports, Shafter wisely concluded that only veteran regular troops would embark. Since there were not quite enough regulars to fill the transports, he decided to send along with the regulars two volunteer regiments and one half of the volunteer dismounted cavalry, the Rough Riders.

He ordered his colonels to board their regiments on any available transport during the three days to follow and trusted their individual initiative to find shipping space for their troops. Because of inadequate shipping capacity only seventeen thousand officers and men embarked and many, many tons of supplies were left ashore. Thousands of disappointed volunteer military personnel were left in Florida, never to see any kind of military action.

On arriving at Port Tampa, the black Twenty-fifth Infantry Regiment boarded the steamer *Concho,* a freighter that had been hurriedly remodeled into a troop ship. The *Concho* was a large ship, but, as it had been hastily refitted for wartime service, comforts were lacking. Four tiers of bunks of undressed lumber, each surrounded by a railing six inches high, filled the space from the floor to the ceiling. In such a bunk a soldier had to keep himself, his personal belongings and his rifle. The ship provided one toilet for every 1,256 men. One would certainly not expect the transport to be a three star cruise ship, but it was definitely crude and uncomfortable beyond acceptable standards.

Confusion reigned as to the loading of the transports. The Fourth U.S. Infantry had preceded the Twenty-fifth Infantry aboard the *Concho*, and on the following day a battalion of the Second Massachusetts Volunteers tried to squeeze onto the ship, causing so much crowding that the late arrivals went ashore to travel on another vessel.

The aggressiveness of both Colonel Wood and Roosevelt, however, paid off. Their Rough Riders embarked for Cuba by seizing, boarding, and holding an unguarded transport that others thought had been designated for them. In a triumph of chutzpah, Colonel Wood "borrowed" a small boat and headed out into the harbor to commandeer the transport *Yucatan*. Asked by the ship's skipper what his authority was, he replied "by orders of General Shafter" and directed that the troop ship be brought to the dock.

Roosevelt had been instructed to have the troops ready for boarding, in order that they could board quickly as soon as the ship touched the dock. Marching his troops past the waiting soldiers of the Seventy-first New York Volunteer Infantry, Roosevelt took possession of the gangway. When the volunteers' officer, who outranked Lieutenant Colonel Roosevelt, demanded that he relinquish his position and pull his troops back, Roosevelt filibustered and detained the volunteers and their officers long enough to allow Colonel Wood to arrive with the transport. At that point, Colonel Wood was ranking officer; he prevailed and loaded his troops first. The other troops took what space was left, quarters so small that only eight companies (about five hundred soldiers) of the Rough Riders sailed to Cuba.

Almost one hundred years later, in an age of total integration of the armed forces, it is amusing to picture the challenge that confronted those in command of the troops embarking for Cuba when the realization struck them that black and white troops occupied the same transports. Telegraph lines between Tampa and Washington must have become overheated with recriminations and accusations about the lack of foresight on the part of the high command in letting the two races embark on the same ships. Even a minimal amount of planning could have prevented this "dreadful" integration of the troops in such close quarters, but the problem was overlooked and whites and blacks had to suffer each others' presence in great intimacy.

Segregation, the stark political reality of the time, undoubtedly did pose a thorny problem with each commanding officer arriving at his own solution to the challenge of keeping the races separate. Some ships were segregated from side to side, with blacks on one side and whites on the other; while other ships had a top-to-bottom segregation: blacks occupying the bottom decks and whites the top decks. Fortunately for the black Twenty-fifth Infantry, their ship was segregated from side to side by assigning the white Fourth Infantry to the port side and the blacks the starboard. Letters written by black soldiers after the hostilities state that, during the sea voyage, black troops were not allowed on deck except with special permission.

When the *Concho* did finally reach the open sea, an order was issued by the brigade commander directing that the two regiments on board the ship, one white and the other black, should not mix. This is ironic since, having served together in Montana when the army was used to restore order during labor union strife, the personnel of the two regiments were on the best of terms.

All of the converted freighters bulged with troops and supplies as the fleet finally moved out into Tampa Bay. Progress, however, was suddenly halted when the army received orders from Washington to delay its departure and not move into the open sea because of an unconfirmed sighting of two Spanish warships lying in wait for them. The soldiers, together with the mules (some of which died), remained on board the transports, which docked for six days in Tampa Bay until orders came again to embark on the open sea. Of the one thousand black men on board the *Concho*, none was allowed to go ashore unless an officer took a whole company at one time to bathe and exercise, a practice probably reflective of the unease created in the minds of the officers by the riot on that last night in Tampa. Other vessels permitted their men to go ashore at any time they chose, while, as would be expected, troops of the Rough Riders were allowed liberal shore leave during the wait. The incarceration aboard ship resulted in almost intolerable hardship, because lack of ventilation in the ship's holds made sleeping below unbearable.

A large number of the only available seats on the main deck

of the *Concho* had been reserved for officers, and a sentinel was posted on each side to keep soldiers from using them. Another order directed that the white regiment be allowed to make coffee first each day, with a guard being detailed to be certain that this order was carried out. The writer of this particular report, a soldier of the Twenty-fifth Infantry, felt that these restrictions were probably imposed to humiliate the blacks and noted that there was no word of protest from their officers. These men suffered without complaint.

After fear of attack by Spanish warships had abated, the expeditionary forces finally sailed on June 14. Three black women, three soldiers, and the dock stevedores were the only persons on the dock to bid farewell to the first significant expeditionary force in American history, setting out for a distant, tropical disease-infested shore with an inadequate number of men and grossly inadequate equipment.

The ship *Leona*, on which Pershing and the black Tenth Cavalry traveled, had some twelve hundred men crowded below deck. Although the cavalrymen were allowed topside whenever they chose, they had been assigned to the lower decks which had six-foot ceilings above three tiers of hammocks occupied by two men at a time. Only two ventilation shafts provided fresh air circulation, and there were only twelve toilets for the entire regiment.

Extremely hot weather continued as the convoy crept slowly toward the southeast until finally the Dry Tortugas were sighted on June 15, and the north coast of Cuba came into view on Sunday, June 18. By then the soldiers had entered the Windward

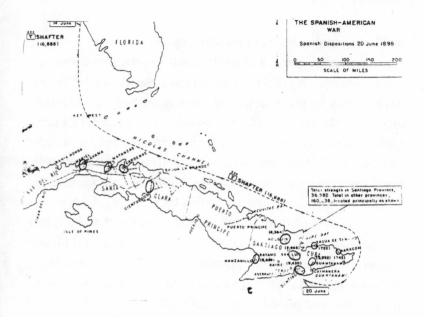

This diagram shows the path of Shafter's forces from Florida to Santiago, Cuba, and the principal locations of the Spanish forces as of June 20, 1898.

Passage still not knowing exactly where they were destined to land, but a short time later they saw the mountains that surround the city of Santiago de Cuba, so they concluded that this was their destination.

On June 20 and 21, the invasion fleet off the coast of Cuba, consisting of thirty-five transports and fourteen warships, wallowed and circled on the line, pitching and rolling in a moderately rough sea that caused discomfort and seasickness. Orders of June 21 stated that the first contingent of troops would disembark the following morning at about ten o'clock, following a preliminary two-hour bombardment of the coast by the navy.

Although General Miles was Commanding General of the United States Army, his ideas on how the war should be carried out had been for the most part ignored. A nagging Cassandra, he urged that the attack on Cuba should not be undertaken until after the rainy season that extends through the spring and summer months. By October the rains stop and clear weather prevails. Since his advice was not taken, the invading American troops would face appalling obstacles caused by recurring deluges that made trails and roads frightfully muddy and rivers and streams turbulent and wide. Inordinate physical hardship caused by wet equipment and wet woolen clothing would add to the troubles of the overburdened troops. The wet conditions made the movement of men and materials so difficult that it is probable that the army would have been defeated had it not had valiant, determined warriors with good leadership. It was fortunate that it faced a Spanish foe whose forces, although significantly outnumbering the Americans, were so widely deployed that troop concentrations were not heavy enough at any location to put up a sufficiently determined resistance. The Americans were also lucky that a hurricane did not blow them away, since the invasion took place during the hurricane season.

General Shafter, learning before the invasion that he was free to select the site at which he would disembark his troops, planned to capture the hills above Santiago and not to march on the fortified positions at the mouth of Santiago Harbor as the navy had wished. He did not submit his plans to Admiral Sampson of the United States Navy, who was expecting the American troops to open the Spanish harbor by reducing the artillery fortifications at the mouth of the harbor. The navy was eager to carry the battle to the enemy but could not do so while the Spanish navy was protected by the shore batteries of Santiago. General Shafter's differing strategy was to control Santiago from the hills above the harbor and flush out the Spanish fleet by bombardment from the hills.

The United States Navy had aspired to block the narrow, shallow channel at the entrance to Santiago Harbor by sinking the old iron warship, *Merrimac,* in the harbor entrance in order to obstruct the channel and keep the large Spanish warships from passing out of the harbor. If this could have been accomplished, the harbor exit could then have been patrolled by much smaller American warships. Valiant Commodore Richard Hobson, with seven volunteer sailors, almost succeeded in sinking the old collier in the narrowest part of the channel. They were thwarted by tidal currents that proved too strong and by enemy fire that destroyed the *Merrimac*'s steering gear, causing the ship to sink in the wrong place where it did not obstruct the harbor. Commodore Schley, a witness to the heroism of Hobson and his men, described the action: "They went through a perfect hell of fire on him and his men. They went into the Jaws of death. It was Balaklava all over again, without the means of defense the light brigade had." Had Hobson been successful, his exploit would have freed a large segment of the main United States fleet to cross the Atlantic and attack the shores and harbors of continental Spain.[14]

Invasion of a hostile shore is a formidable task, especially when there are not enough small vessels to land the troops.

Fortunately, the navy provided steam launches that pulled to the shore groups of small boats filled with men and equipment. It seems incredible that during this operation only two soldiers drowned (after falling into deep water while heavily laden with equipment). Only two lighters, one of which became disabled, were available for carrying supplies and weapons; so a significant portion of much needed equipment never made it ashore. In the nethermost regions of the ships, over two thousand horses and mules had been loaded. The mules had been brought to pull the 114 six-mule army wagons, the eighty-one escort supply wagons and the seven ambulances, of which only a few ever reached shore. The horses were for the use of those officers who chose to ride, but horseback riding proved difficult due to the terrain and the presence of barbed wire entanglements on the battlefields. The most efficient way to get the horses ashore proved to be simply pushing the beasts into the surf; although this so depleted the supply of mules that only about one-half of the needed number reached shore. Fifty mules and horses decided to swim back to Tampa, but the majority were controlled by tying ropes to their halters and pulling them ashore.[15]

Shafter's confidence in the abilities of black regular soldiers, developed during his service with them in the West, is undoubtedly reflected in the fact that the initial invasion force consisted of the Ninth and Tenth cavalries and the Twenty-fifth Infantry, plus the Rough Riders of Teddy Roosevelt. The landing was at Daiquiri, a small village which later became famous for the drink named after it. Accessible by a small road about seven miles down the coast was the small port of Siboney where the remainder of the troopships unloaded. The invading army consisted of 14,935 regular infantry and 803 officers. In addition, there were twelve companies of dismounted cavalry and one company of cavalry with horses. All troops invading Cuba were members of regular army units except the First Volunteer Cavalry (Rough Riders), the Volunteer Seventy-first New York Infantry, and the Second Volunteer Massachusetts Infantry.

8

Our God and Soldiers we alike adore,
Ev'n at the Brink of danger, not before:
After deliverance, both alike required;
Our God's forgotten, and our Soldiers slighted.

—Francis Quarles

Leaders of the Invasion and Their Weapons

The small but professional army invading Cuba was fortunate in having a collection of leaders who were veterans of the Civil War. All except General Joseph Wheeler had also faced the rigors of duty in the West and had led troops against the Indians. General Wheeler had missed Indian fighting because his service in the Confederate army had disqualified him from wearing the bluecoat of the United States Army after the South had been defeated, and it was only in early 1898 that the president reinstated him as an officer in the army.

While fighting the Indians, each of the regular army officers leading invasion forces had spent some of his career in charge of black soldiers and therefore was no stranger to their superb fighting capabilities. While the period for preparing troops for war had been very short, the commanding officers had the traits of character and experience necessary to overcome the problems presented by weather, inadequate artillery and supplies, and the too-brief period allowed to mold their organizations into smoothly operating military units.

The officer corps of the army at that time was so small that those who did have positions of leadership had served together on many previous occasions. Close relationships had been established, either at West Point, during the Civil War or in the West fighting Indians. This prior service had fortified that mutual confidence so essential to developing strategy and perfecting tactics. From battlefield experiences each knew the strengths of the others, so was able to evaluate and keep in perspective the leadership capacities or flaws of each of his colleagues.

General Matthew Ridgeway later expressed his feelings about leadership: " . . . I hold that leadership is not a science, but an art. It conceives an ideal, states it as an objective, and then seeks actively and earnestly to attain it, everlastingly persevering, because the records of war are full of successes coming to those leaders who stuck it out just a little longer than their opponents."

The attacking American forces, all members of the Fifth Army Corps, had been divided into two divisions of infantry and one of cavalry. General Shafter had been appointed to command the invading army, but events would prove that without the skill and fighting instincts of his subordinate officers the events of the next two weeks would have turned into a military disaster.

General Joseph Wheeler had been appointed commander of the First Cavalry Division that was to attack the eastern slope of

San Juan Hill, and General Henry W. Lawton was in command of the First Infantry Division, whose military objective was to capture the hilltop fortifications at El Caney. General Jacob E. Kent was to lead the Second Infantry Division in its assault on the southern flank of San Juan Hill, joining forces with the cavalry division in this attack.

General William R. Shafter

General William R. Shafter had volunteered for duty in the Civil War, and after the Civil War had chosen to remain in the regular army. From his experience in the Indian Wars that followed, Shafter grew to be considered one of the most capable and energetic senior officers in the Army. He was particularly familiar with the special attributes of black cavalry and black infantry units. From the pool of veterans of both the Civil War and the Indian Wars, officers had been selected to lead troops in Cuba. Largely due to his seniority in the military ranks, the army had chosen General Shafter, sixty-two years old (three years from mandatory retirement) to lead the military expedition and to command the invasion forces.

Shafter's personal appearance was deceptive. Although he was a huge man, huge to the point of obesity, he was nonetheless an experienced, disciplined, and decisive leader who knew how to delegate authority. His post-war reputation suffered as the result of an ongoing feud with newspaper correspondents, causing him to receive a bad press that influenced both the public's attitude toward him and the opinions of future historians assessing the war. Since his largest command had been of a regiment, his most serious shortcoming and the easiest to criticize was his lack of experience in handling large numbers of troops.

Colonel Shafter, called "Pecos Bill," had been assigned to Fort Davis, Texas, in 1872 and was considered one of the most colorful officers ever assigned there. In 1867, construction of Fort Davis near the Mexican border had enabled the Army to patrol the road connecting San Antonio with Santa Fe. The history of Fort Davis from 1867 to 1881 is the story of white officers and their four black regiments stationed there (the Ninth and Tenth Cavalries and the Twenty-fourth and Twenty-fifth Infantries). In 1878, companies of the Tenth Cavalry and the Twenty-fifth Infantry stationed at Fort Davis totalled 6,724 miles of scouting mileage, the most of any unit in Texas. Shafter's most remarkable exploit, one that sheds light on his character, was an expedition he made into the "badlands" of the southeastern corner of New Mexico, called "The Staked Plains." With sixty-three black troopers he pursued a band of Indians for weeks through the desert-like territory, sometimes traveling seventy miles a day without water. After twenty-two days in the field he returned, having failed in his efforts to catch the wily Indians; however, the exploit was of great value because he brought back geographical knowledge of the unexplored desert and proved to the Indians that because of the white man's tenacity and determination the area could no longer be a sanctuary for marauders.

During the battles in Cuba, Shafter gave directions and participated in staff meetings while stretched out on a wooden door, undoubtedly to relieve the pressure on his back caused by his obesity. When stirring himself enough to view the battleground from an observation post or to attend a meeting, he always rode a mule rather than a horse. It must have been an exceptional mule (later he was hoisted onto the saddle of a horse to participate in the formal surrender ceremonies). William Randolph Hearst, reporting on the war in Cuba, described General Shafter as "a bold lion-headed hero, and massive as to body—a sort of human fortress in blue coat and flannel shirt."

General Joseph Wheeler

With a thin frame of only five-feet-five-inches in height, General Joseph Wheeler, age sixty-one, in contrast to Shafter looked to be a slight physical specimen. His seeming frailness was accentuated by a full white beard and thick snow-white hair, but his appearance was in truth deceptive. Within that thin body was a vigorous, athletic man whose fighting spirit had earned him, during the Civil War, the sobriquet "Fighting Joe Wheeler." Events to follow at Las Guasimas and on San Juan Hill proved him to have an entirely appropriate nickname.

Wheeler graduated from the United States Military Academy in 1859 and became a distinguished cavalry leader in the Confederate Army, attaining the rank of lieutenant general when only twenty-eight years of age. After the war, failing to get a commission in the United States Army, he re-entered politics to serve as a distinguished and fiery Congressman from Alabama.

So desirous was Wheeler of leading troops in the impending war that he had a personal interview with President McKinley to request that he be given a commission in the Army. Like any skilled politician, McKinley realized that to appoint Wheeler to a position of leadership would please his Southern constituents, so he appointed him a major general in the cavalry. Later, in the heat of the Battle of Las Guasimas, Wheeler was heard to refer to the Spaniards as "Damn Yankees."

For the first time in more than thirty-eight years, the old Confederate officer donned the blue United States Army uniform and became so emotionally attached to it that later he requested to be buried in it. At Wheeler's funeral, an old Confederate comrade-at-arms, standing beside his coffin, was heard to say, "I hate to think of what old Stonewall's going to say when he sees you arrivin' in that old uniform."

Wheeler's division consisted of fewer than 2,500 dismounted cavalrymen, of which the vast majority were regular troops of the black Ninth and Tenth cavalries and the white First, Third, and Sixth cavalries. Added to these veterans were the five hundred volunteer Rough Riders, one of whom was General Wheeler's oldest son, an 1895 graduate of West Point.

General Henry W. Lawton

Henry W. Lawton was born nineteen years before the start of the Civil War, in which he enlisted as a private in the Union Army. He had been promoted within a short time to lieutenant and then quickly to lieutenant colonel. In the Atlanta campaign he had been awarded the Medal of Honor for gallantry.

After a brief period in Harvard School of Law, he had rejoined the army as a second lieutenant in 1866 and was assigned to an outfit of black soldiers that was transformed into the Twenty-fourth Infantry when the army was reorganized after the

Civil War. As an Indian fighter and as a commander of troops in the field, his career was exceptional and had shown much promise for his future in the Army. Lawton, well over six feet tall, was a dynamic, handsome, muscular man who radiated enthusiasm. The most remarkable exploit in his military history was a thirteen hundred-mile pursuit of the Apache chieftain, Geronimo, who had led him on a chase through Arizona and Mexico before surrendering. By the onset of the war in Cuba he had risen to the rank of major general and had been placed in charge of the First Infantry Division.

Later, while on duty in the Philippines, Lawton brought his wife and large number of children to live in Manila. This proved especially tragic for his family because, shortly after their arrival, the general's promising career ended when he was shot through the heart by a Filipino in December 1899. Lawton, Oklahoma, is named in his honor.

General Jacob Ford Kent

General Kent, born in Philadelphia in 1835, lived to the ripe age of eighty-three years. Attending West Point for five years, he graduated in 1861. As an officer in the Civil War he had a variety of experiences, including spending time in a Confederate prison camp from which he was released in a prisoner swap. On rejoining his outfit, there was still plenty of fighting to do in the battles of Antietam, Falmouth, and Fredericksburg. Although he had been promoted to the rank of brevet colonel, his rank reverted to that of major after the war.

Following several years on garrison duty in the defeated

South, he had been sent to fight the Indians in the upper plains, where the onset of the Spanish-American War found him, at age sixty-three a full colonel in charge of the black Twenty-fourth Infantry. For some reason, Shafter had developed a lack of confidence in General Kent. Despite this, Shafter made him commander, possibly due to his seniority, of the Second Infantry Division, whose mission was to attack the Spanish fortifications on the southern slopes of San Juan Hill.

None of the regiments of the three divisions of the Fifth Army had ever participated in joint training maneuvers, so their being thrown together in one army corps was purely a matter of chance. It was therefore even more imperative that junior officers accept increased responsibility in the forthcoming battles, and, fortunately, they did so.

During the Battle of San Juan Hill, General Kent had become diverted from his primary mission by the apparent cowardice of the Seventy-first New York Volunteers and was not available to order his troops to begin the assault up the hill. His subordinate, General Hawkins, later criticized his absence because the full responsibility of initiating the charge fell upon Hawkins. Kent was also the later object of bitter recrimination by the New Yorkers for his testimony about their panic when under fire. Following the cessation of hostilities, Kent was promoted to the rank of major general and retired in October 1898.

Colonel Leonard Wood

A man of many talents, Colonel Leonard Wood was a physician who had graduated from Harvard Medical School. Not satisfied with serving only as a physician to sick and wounded soldiers, Wood had commanded troops in battle against the Indians in Arizona. He had served with distinction in the West, leading troops against the Apaches, and had discharged his duty so heroically that he had been awarded the Medal of Honor.

At the completion of the Indian Wars he had been transferred to Washington where he served as the personal physician to President McKinley and Secretary of War Alger. Wood had persuaded his friend Theodore Roosevelt to use his influence to find him a position in a fighting outfit for service in the Cuban campaign. Roosevelt was able to persuade New York congressman William Astor Chandler to arrange a commission for both himself and his friend Leonard Wood.

Wood was so highly regarded by the authorities in Washington that after the peace treaty was signed he was appointed military governor of Cuba, a post he held for two years. When the Cubans had drawn up their new constitution and held elections he returned to the States.

Weapons of the War

In weaponry the United States was on unequal footing: the Spanish army possessed the more advanced, Belgian-manufactured, bolt-action Mauser rifle. The Mauser rifle, firing smokeless powder, was so effective that by 1900 it had become the prototype for infantry weapons throughout Europe. While both Spanish artillery and infantry used smokeless powder, the unlucky volunteer soldiers in the American army were forced to use the obsolete black powder ammunition fired by the Springfield rifle that emitted a large cloud of whitish smoke, betraying their position each time they fired.

The volunteer American soldiers not only would have their positions betrayed each time they fired, they had the further disadvantage of having had little training in the proper aiming and firing of the Springfield rifle that had been issued to them. Using a Springfield rifle, an uninstructed soldier, failing to adjust the sight of his gun properly, might think he was aiming accurately at an enemy but observe his bullet strike the ground six hundred yards short of the mark. All volunteer troops suffered this disadvantage, except, of course, the Rough Riders who were issued new Krag-Jorgensen weapons.

The United States Army did have enough modern weapons, however, to equip their regular troops with these new Krag-Jorgensen rifles that used smokeless powder cartridges. The regular army troops, experienced in fighting Indians and armed with the Krag-Jorgensen rifles, prided themselves on their good marksmanship. General Wheeler was impressed by the regular soldiers who "could estimate distances with wonderful accuracy" and, in addition to being superbly drilled, were "expert marksmen to a wonderful degree." In battle their fire was most deadly and effective. In his report on the Santiago campaign, General Wheeler stated: "Many of the Rough Riders were also good marksmen, but they had not been drilled to use the kind of rifles with which they were armed; and it is also true that many of them had never fired a rifle of any kind in their lives, and, while they went forward with courage and determination, their fire was not as effective as that of the regulars."

The technology of artillery was likewise undergoing many changes during the last quarter of the nineteenth century.[16] Concurrent with modifications in artillery weapons themselves was a dramatic improvement in the manufacture of gunpowder. In 1886, a French chemist, Vieille, introduced his "poudre B," produced by combining gunpowder with a mixture of gelatin. When the compound dried and hardened it could be rolled into cords that gave off no smoke as it burned steadily, giving rise to the first smokeless powder from which cordite was developed for use in artillery and later in rifles. By 1896, as a filling for explosive shells, gunpowder had become obsolete for all European armies. In contrast, the effectiveness of American artillery was limited because the army still had many muzzle loaders that fired black powder whose cloud of white smoke disclosed their location to the enemy. Aiming American artillery pieces was difficult because range finders for accurately pinpointing a target were not available; so the target had to be in full view before it could be engaged. In the forests of hilly Cuba, American artillery was ineffective if the target lay more than a thousand yards distant, a range no greater than that of artillery used in the Civil War.

While the American navy had been equipped with the latest in heavy weapons, it had to reconcile itself to a severe shortage of smokeless powder since it had almost depleted the small supply that had accompanied one of its new ships constructed in a European country. An article in the *New York Times* stated that warships in the American navy were obliged to use ordinary powder rather than the smokeless variety with which all European armies and navies had been fully stocked. The paper indicated that most criticism for the shortage should be directed toward Admiral Sampson, since he had been head of the Bureau of Ordnance for the prior three years.

Probably the most preposterous decision made by Shafter or his superiors was to bring with the expedition a siege train that was extremely heavy and so difficult to load on a transport that the wharf broke while it was being loaded. Being a train, it needed a track to give it mobility while ashore, but the only port with a railroad was at Caimanera, on the west cost of Guantanamo Bay, forty miles east of Santiago, with no connecting roads. In spite of everything, the siege train with its guns was reported to have been landed on the beach at Daiquiri on July 3, but it was never used.

Because of an inadequate transport system for the invading American forces, artillery, that essential element of any modern well-equipped army, was in very short supply, a deficiency that almost proved disastrous for the attacking forces. Due to the shortage of shipping space on the transports, six of the ten batteries of field artillery assembled in Tampa were left in Florida; so only four seven-inch howitzers and four five-inch siege guns were available for the assaults on the heavily fortified hills of El Caney and San Juan Ridge.

It is not surprising that the deficiency of artillery pieces proved to be a serious obstacle to the Americans' ability to effectively attack the summits of the well-protected Spanish hilltop fortifications, a shortage that was later reflected in the very high percentage of casualties among those assaulting the crests of the hills. Moreover, since their artillery weapons expelled large clouds of smoke when fired, the Americans were at a serious disadvantage because the enemy, from their elevated fortifications, could easily locate the artillery emplacements. Of the heavy ordnance accompanying the invasion forces, the four Gatling machine guns probably proved more valuable than any other heavy weapons. The rapid-firing Gatlings were used in an unconventional manner and proved their effectiveness during the assault up San Juan Hill.[17]

9

But when the blast of war blows in our ears . . .

—Shakespeare, *King Henry V*

Invasion of Cuba

By evening of June 22, 1898, most of the Second Infantry Division and part of the cavalry division had set foot on foreign soil. It was fortunate that this landing had no opposition, for it seems obvious in retrospect that minimal resistance could have easily repulsed it. This was the first of a number of remarkably fortuitous circumstances that led to the success of this poorly conceived and executed military venture in a hostile tropical country.

A motley group of soldiers of the Cuban insurgent army emerged from the jungle to meet the American invasion forces shortly after their landing. The pathetic appearance of the ragged army that lined up to welcome them caused much sympathy and pity among the American troops. In addition to providing information about Spanish troop deployment, Cuban insurgents proved of great value as guides through the jungle trails to the Spanish strongholds. Most of the shabby fellows were coatless and shoeless, and many had clothing so badly torn that they were almost nude; however, their weapons, ammunition, and machetes seemed well maintained. The insurgent Cubans proved to be a mixed blessing, because, although providing essential scouting and jungle guide services for the army, they had a propensity for stealing anything not securely fastened. Equipment temporarily laid aside by overburdened American troops, sweating and stumbling in their advance through the jungle, usually disappeared within a short time. At the Battle of Las Guasimas, a few days later, everything that had been put aside by the American troops for the duration of the battle—including food rations—disappeared into the clutches of the ravenous horde of insurgent Cuban troops. Such theft not only seriously jeopardized the effectiveness of the Americans, but completely alienated the American troops toward the Cuban insurgent troops.

General Shafter ordered his army to push forward without delay. After halting long enough to be certain that all men were present, they marched from Daiquiri to Siboney down an old road into the jungles of Cuba. The black Twenty-fifth Infantry had the honor of leading the march to Siboney from the landing site at Daiquiri on the first day the army invaded the island. Since there had been no opposition to the landing, the Americans moved inland where the real opposition proved to be the impenetrable jungle that could not be pierced except by cutting through with machetes, a piece of equipment foreign to the ordinary American soldier. So thick was the jungle that it was necessary for the first landing force to follow the advice of the Cubans and use the existing seven miles of trails to reach the coastal town of Siboney. Progress through the jungle was made especially difficult by many prior days of rainfall that had made the trails extremely muddy. Heat, wet clothing, and swarms of mosquitoes and other insects added to their discomfort as they trudged along the narrow trail through dense wilderness; but the distress caused by the environment was not as bad as the more intense suffering from thirst due to a shortage of potable water. At Siboney, where they found a favorable beach and dock for completion of troop landings, they were also able to relieve their thirst. Siboney had been a small military stronghold that could easily have been defended by the five hundred Spanish troops occupying it shortly before the invasion, but the Spanish had decided to abandon it and its excellent fortifications.

Adding to the worries of American leaders was the known presence of a large contingent of thousands of well-equipped Spanish soldiers hurrying to reinforce Santiago from the west. Shafter had heard that General Escoria was approaching Santiago from the west with some eight thousand troops when in reality it was General Pando, with only thirty-seven hundred men, who was struggling through the jungle and the Cuban resistance forces. So large was the reported contingent of Spanish reinforcements that the Americans judged it even more urgent to attack Santiago before their expected arrival on either July 3 or July 4. Consequently, the American army landed during the rainy season in a miasmic, swampy jungle, so impenetrable that one could traverse only previously cut trails. Their objective was to attack an experienced enemy concealed in well-fortified, elevated positions. It is true that General Shafter had thought it desirable to quickly engage the enemy and to overcome him without loss of time; however, he was as unaware as his superiors that the expedition had only a brief window of opportunity before the forces of nature would cut them down and reduce them to a feeble military force whose effectiveness would be completely destroyed by disease.

More than two weeks spent packed into the hold of a suffocating, poorly ventilated troop ship would make even the most timid soldier welcome a chance to escape from his iron-walled, floating prison to cavort on the beach and in the cool surf of even a hostile, threatening tropical country whose jungle at any moment might erupt with vicious rifle fire from a brutal foe. The euphoria and excitement generated by completion of a difficult, miserable ocean voyage led the last contingent of invading troops to throw caution to the winds and make a jolly festivity of their disembarkation. Under naval searchlights the last of the invasion force landed at night on the beach at Siboney. The disembarkation was described by one of the soldiers: "It was one of the most weird and remarkable scenes of the war, probably of any war. An army was being landed on an enemy's coast at the dead of night, but with somewhat more of cheers and shrieks and laughter than rise from the bathers in the surf at Coney Island on a hot Sunday. It was a pandemonium of noises. The men still to be landed from the 'prison hulks,' as they called the transports, were singing in chorus; the men already on shore were dancing naked around the camp fires on the beach . . . . On either side rose black, overhanging ridges; in the lowland between were white tents and burning fires, and from the ocean came the blazing, dazzling eyes of the searchlights."

What sort of enemy was the unseasoned American Army getting ready to meet? For three years there had been a serious insurrection in Cuba in which the Cuban people (largely black), having risen up against their Spanish overlords, had waged continuous guerrilla warfare.[18] Spain had sent some of its best troops to the island, arming them well with modern weapons, and they had had a chance to become acclimated to Cuba. Spanish veterans, experienced in the art of war, knew how to fortify strategic locations, post snipers, dig trenches and handle their modern artillery with precision. Such troops were no push-overs, so the Americans were taking a great risk in thinking they could defeat the Spanish soldiers in their own territory where they had had adequate time to prepare.

On the other hand, Spanish forces, demoralized by delays in pay, poor food, and the constant pressure of warfare against a determined insurgent foe, faced the onslaught of a yellow fever epidemic whose horrors were just beginning to become evident. Thus occurred yet another episode in a chain of fortuitous events that unmanned the Spanish and weakened their physical and mental powers, just at the time of the invasion and before the Americans had an opportunity to be affected by the disease. Such factors undoubtedly contributed to a lack of aggressiveness on the part of the Spanish, who actually confined their activities to defense of their existing strongholds.

The Spaniards had developed a devilishly clever method of posting snipers at strategic spots to do maximum damage to the enemy. Possibly they had learned the technique from the Cuban rebels with whom they had been fighting for years. Snipers climbed palm trees where they camouflaged themselves among the leaves, and after tieing themselves in a comfortable position, they were able to remain at their posts for many hours. Frequently they wore heavy green jackets whose large pockets were filled with sand to make a kind of bulletproof vest. From their elevated, camouflaged positions they were able to fire down on American troops without being seen. Such snipers created havoc among the Americans, both at Las Guasimas and at San Juan Hill, by remaining in the trees even after the principal battles had been concluded, continuing to pick off the wounded, any stragglers, and those returning to the coast for supplies. Colonel Wood of the Rough Riders later stated that guerrillas in trees had seemed to devote themselves especially to shooting at surgeons, hospital assistants with Red Cross badges on their arms, the wounded carried on litters, and burying parties. After the main Battle of San Juan Hill, a detachment of American snipers was sent along the trail to the coast and was able to kill thirteen of their Spanish counterparts.

10

He is out of bounds now
He rejoices in man's lovely
peculiar power to choose life and die—
when he leads his black soldiers to death,
he cannot bend his back.

—Robert Lowell

The Battle of Las Guasimas

The first battle of the Cuban campaign took place on June 24, 1898, at a place called Las Guasimas (named for a clump of guasima, or hog nut, trees at that location) that was the juncture of the road between Siboney on the coast and Santiago. Some historians have called the battle an ambush, but it is best described as a delaying action by the Spaniards, who were under orders to retire if the pressure became too great. The skillful and energetic involvement of the black Tenth Cavalry, over one-quarter of the total number of troops involved in the battle, was fundamental to forcing the Spanish to retreat, since the undermanned Rough Riders did not have enough firepower or experience to make a successful advance toward the fort.

The battle was a preliminary Spanish defensive effort to test

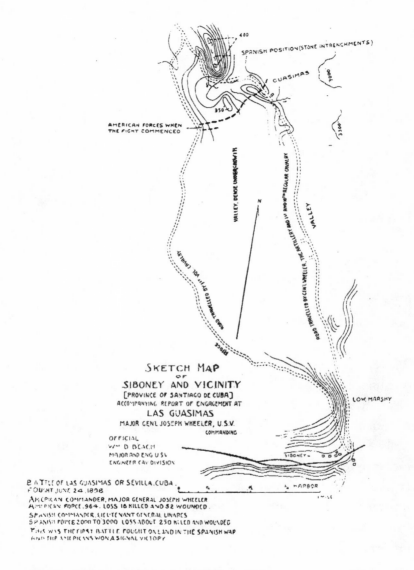

Sketch of Siboney and vicinity showing positions
at the battle of Las Guisamas.

the mettle of the attacking troops. Whether Spanish plans included encirclement and destruction of the small American force is unknown, but it is reasonable to assume that, if they could have surrounded the Americans, they would have made the effort to wipe them out.

In warfare, troops that have been properly trained are highly motivated and eager to engage the enemy without delay. When man's deep-seated aggressive instinct has been brought to a fever-pitch, as it is in warfare, it is imperative that confrontation with the enemy be undertaken as quickly as possible. As with countless leaders of warriors since men first began fighting one another, an unspoken rivalry existed between the various American troop commanders as to who would be the first to engage the enemy in combat.

On the morning of June 24, the First Volunteer Cavalry, generally known as the Rough Riders, happened to be the lead regiment in the advance. General Wheeler, in command of the entire cavalry division, had earned a reputation for exceptional aggressiveness in the Civil War. He had the sudden inspiration to take what few cavalry troops he had available at the moment and advance inland to be the first to meet the enemy face-to-face. However, General Shafter had entrusted command of the advance into the jungles of Cuba to an officer of known reliability, General Lawton, who was outranked by General Wheeler.

General Lawton had given no orders to his subordinates to move north toward the enemy; so, in the absence of explicit orders from any superior, General Wheeler decided to order his small group of cavalry to leave before daybreak to seek battle with the Spaniards. To accomplish this, and to avoid the possibility of receiving orders contrary to his plan, he directed the troops to evade Lawton at Siboney and to set up camp in a beautiful coconut grove a short distance inland from the town. Only half of the Rough Riders (approximately 250 men, the other half being bivouacked on the beach preparing for the trek to Santiago) assembled at the camp under the direct command of Colonel Leonard Wood, with Roosevelt second in command. Adding to the assemblage were one squadron from the First Cavalry Regiment and a second from the black Tenth Cavalry Regiment, which gave Wheeler a force of just under one thousand men. Wheeler decided that he had enough manpower to accomplish his goal. At 3:30 a.m., the contingent of neophyte and regular soldiers started inland along two separate trails at a rapid pace, urged forward by enthusiastic officers.

From the outskirts of Siboney, the northwest road leading inland to Santiago divided into two branches. The eastern branch left the beach by way of a low, marshy gap in the coastal hills and crossed a valley covered with dense undergrowth before climbing a small coastal mountain range approximately three miles from the coast. General Wheeler and the regular cavalry soldiers (squadrons of the First and Tenth Regular Cavalry) took this eastern branch of the road with plans to meet the Rough Riders at Las Guasimas, where the two segments of the road intersected some four miles inland from the coast. A pass in the mountain range traversed by a creek was located at this intersection of the roads.

The Rough Riders started inland up the western segment of

the road from Siboney, taking a route that was actually nothing more than a tortuous trail that later joined the eastern branch at the gap in the coastal range. They immediately had to ascend a ridge, along whose summit the trail ran inland to that gap in the coastal ridges where the two trails converged. At a point three miles inland the trail had on its eastern side a collection of hills, one of which was 350 feet high, and just to the north of that point, where the two roads converged, was a second hill on which the Spanish had built a small stone fort to protect the pass.

The inexperienced Rough Riders, invading a foreign country, marching through dense jungle to meet an experienced, well-armed foe, seemed to have no awareness of the gravity of the situation. War correspondent and novelist Stephen Crane was able to catch up with the rear of the Rough Riders' column and was surprised at the casualness of their attitude. "They wound along this narrow winding path, babbling joyously, arguing, recounting, and laughing; making more noise than a train going through a tunnel."

On the prior day's reconnaissance, Colonel Wood, in command of the Rough Riders, had been warned by Cuban insurgents that Spanish soldiers were deployed along the road to oppose the inland advance of the Americans. The Americans had also learned from the insurgents' General Castillo that the Spanish planned to resist the advance inland. General Castillo had even given them a map with a description of the Spanish position on the Santiago road. The rebels claimed the Spanish outpost could easily be found on the trail because the abandoned body of a dead insurgent soldier lay there. After advancing up the western road at a brisk pace, the Americans encountered the dead soldier. From that point on, Colonel Wood deployed his troops in an attacking line on both sides of the road. So thick was the undergrowth that, once the troops were spread out, it was difficult for any soldier to see more than one or two of his comrades at any time.

Immediately after the American deployment, gunfire from Spanish high-velocity Mauser rifles started whistling and snapping through the trees and underbrush of the jungle around the Rough Riders, who had never before been under hostile fire. The Americans could not tell where to direct an answering fire, since the firing seemed to be coming from all sides with guns chattering in long bursts and bullets ripping the nearby bushes. The volunteer cavalrymen at first chose to remain hidden in heavy underbrush since to go forward or to retreat would make them easy prey for Spanish fire. The Spaniards, well deployed and camouflaged, had several snipers tied in the uppermost branches of tall palm trees. Crawling through the heavy underbrush, the Americans gradually advanced through the dense vegetation that soon gave way to more open terrain, but the Spanish fire became more accurate as the Americans got closer.

While the neophyte Rough Riders were organizing their slow advance toward the enemy, the regular cavalrymen under General Wheeler were arriving. General Wheeler's troops had left camp earlier than had the Rough Riders and had taken the eastern road that was longer but more easily traveled than the rough trail taken by the Rough Riders, so their arrival at the Spanish positions almost coincided with that of the volunteers. Deploying through the bushes to their left, they were able to make contact with the easternmost squad of the Rough Riders.

Officers then directed the black cavalrymen to first attack two lines of shallow Spanish trenches that had been strengthened by thick parapets, making this the strongest position in the tough Spanish defense. Shouting Comanche war whoops above the din of gunfire, the black regulars then charged the trenches and routed the Spanish who fled up the trail toward their main body of troops. In spite of heavy rifle fire from the Spanish, whose poor marksmanship made an advance possible, a final charge forward was made by all troops, volunteers and regulars. Some three hundred yards from the Spanish fort the brush became thinner, permitting the Americans to advance more rapidly, but by this time the defenders had received orders to retreat. The Spanish retired down the road toward Santiago, taking with them most of their dead and wounded.

Corporal Brown of the Tenth Cavalry manned a Hotchkiss gun that proved very effective in silencing the firing from the Spanish fort. Corporal Brown, a black soldier, was killed in the fight; however, his efforts received little recognition after the battle. Conversely, two members of the Rough Riders, Hamilton Fish, Jr., and Captain A. M. Capron, both killed in action, have been extensively honored. Fish was the grandson of the Secretary of State under President Grant.

Casper Whitney, in *Harper's Monthly* of June 1898, described the action: "The regulars charged up the hill, sweeping over the rifle-pits with their dead Spaniards, and driving the living ones before them—a long way before them, as they fled early in the charge. Though early in the day, the heat prostrated many. The Rough Riders then joined the regulars in pursuing the Spanish across the meadow on either side of the road, but the Spanish had too long a start."

Of the three major battles of the war, the Battle of Las Guasimas was most inaccurately reported by the press. This is understandable, because the rapid move inland initiated by General Wheeler toward early morning battle on June 23 surprised everyone, including the commanding general, Lawton. The vast majority of eager but frustrated correspondents had remained at Siboney during the battle that was witnessed by only three of their group: Stephen Crane of the *New York World*, Richard Harding Davis, and Edward Marshall, who was shot in the back while standing alongside Colonel Wood.

Many sorely disappointed correspondents had missed the first battle of the war, but this did not, it seems, deter them in their reporting. They filed volumes of reports about the battle, much of which had little foundation in fact. Each wounded soldier returning from the battle was extensively queried about his interpretation of events. News reports, confusing and sometimes erroneous, were filed before clear knowledge was available as to precise details of that battle on the mist-shrouded ridges of that coastal mountain range. Most newspapers initially reported that a disaster had befallen the Rough Riders as the result of a Spanish ambush, and it was not until Marshall and the outspoken Davis returned that the true situation was learned. By then it was too late to undo the conviction of many Americans that Roosevelt and Wood had been negligent.

News reports about the engagement are conflicting, some stating that the Spanish were already in retreat before the regular cavalry arrived; however, letters and documents from soldiers involved in the battle state definitely that the Rough Riders were pinned down and under heavy fire as snipers, hidden both in the underbrush and among the high leaves of the palm trees, fired at them from three sides. Certain reports even stated that the Spanish soldiers were about to surround them and close the area of retreat when the black cavalry arrived. Many on the scene concluded that the Rough Riders could not have dislodged the Spanish by themselves, and there was a good chance of very severe losses had they not been reinforced by the First and the Tenth cavalries. Even if the volunteers had been seasoned troops, which they definitely were not, their situation was precarious. It would have been unusual for men who had never been under fire—who had, as recently as three months before, been walking the streets of Manhattan as civilians—to be able to withstand such a well-planned confrontation.

A logical rebuttal to the few reports that the black cavalry troops arrived after the Spanish were already retreating is that the casualty figures indicate otherwise. The Tenth Cavalry, in the thick of the fighting, had two men killed and several wounded. General Lawton, after receiving a courier message requesting help, had dispatched a troop of regulars on the double to give assistance, which possibly accounts for some of the confusion in reports of the battle relating to black cavalry participation. The black Twenty-fifth Infantry had been in the same encampment and had heard the fighting at a distance. Receiving orders to reinforce the beleaguered American troops, the Twenty-fifth Infantry could have reached them within two hours; however, the brigade commander took a wrong turn in marching down the trail toward the scene of battle. After fourteen hours of fruitless marching down jungle trails, the exhausted troops finally returned to where they had started.

Men of Troops B and I of the black Tenth Cavalry won particular praise from their commanders because of gallantry, perfect coolness, and fine discipline under fire. A black cavalryman, witness to the Battle of Las Guasimas, claimed that without these "smoked Yankees" (as they were called by the Spanish) of the Tenth Cavalry, the Rough Riders could not have dislodged the Spaniards by themselves. When the white commander of Troop B of the Tenth Cavalry was injured, command of that troop was then taken over by a black non-commissioned officer, John Buck, who led the unit in its vicious assault that contributed significantly to the defeat of the Spaniards.

Sergeant Buck was one of the first Negro soldiers to assume command of a company during the Cuban campaign. Before the end of the war, however, similar performances by black non-commissioned officers became common.[19] A Spanish officer with the troops that made up the forces that lay in wait for the Americans at Las Guasimas on June 24 later said: "What especially terrified our men was the huge American Negroes. We saw their big, black faces through the underbrush, and they looked like devils. They came forward under our fire as if they didn't the least care about it."

The *Tampa Morning Tribune* of June 26, 1898, published a

dispatch stating that after the battle many of the American casualties had been found to have been shot in the back. These casualties may have been the result of both enemy and friendly fire, based on reports of witnesses.

Sergeant Louis Bowman, a black Tenth Cavalry trooper, spoke of the battle as follows:

> The Rough Riders had gone off in great glee, bantering and good naturedly boasting that they were going to lick the Spaniards without any trouble, and advised us to remain where we were until they returned; that they would bring back some Spanish heads as trophies. When we heard firing in the distance our Captain Capron remarked: 'Someone ahead is doing good work.' However, the firing became so heavy and regular that our officers, without orders, decided to move forward and reconnoiter. When we got where we could see what was going on, we found that the Rough Riders had marched down a sort of canyon between the mountains. The Spaniards had men posted at the entrance and, as soon as the Rough Riders had gone in, had closed up the rear and were firing on the Rough Riders from both the front and the rear. Immediately, the Spaniards in the rear received a volley from our men of the Tenth Cavalry, without a command. The Spaniards were afraid we were going to flank them and rushed out of the ambush in front of the Rough Riders, throwing up their hands and shouting, 'Don't shoot, we are

Cubans.' The Rough Riders, thus, let them escape and gave them a chance to take a better position up ahead. The men were in the tall grass and could not even see each other, and I feared the Rough Riders in the rear shot many of their men in the front, mistaking them for Spanish Soldiers.[20]

After the Tenth Cavalry had fully assessed the situation, they adopted the technique they had employed in fighting the Indians by charging headlong toward the Spaniards shouting Comanche war whoops. Bowman said very forcefully: "I don't think it an exaggeration to say that, if it had not been for the timely aid of the Tenth Cavalry, the Rough Riders would have been exterminated. This is the unanimous opinion, at least, of the men of the Tenth Cavalry."

A corporal standing near Captain Capron and Hamilton Fish, Jr., when they were shot reported on the incident late that day to a reporter for the Associated Press: "They were with the Rough Riders and ran into an ambuscade, though they had been warned of the danger. If it had not been for the Negro Cavalry, the Rough Riders would have been exterminated. I am not a Negro lover. My father fought with Mosby's Rangers, and I was born in the South, but the Negroes saved that fight, and the day will come when General Shafter will give them credit for their bravery."

The Associated Press reported that one of the Spanish wounded at the Battle of Las Guasimas indicated that a considerable part of the damage done to American troops was done by seven-millimeter machine guns manned by seamen, which suggests that the Spaniards may have used some of the crews and weapons from the Spanish navy in their defense of the pass traversing the range of coastal mountains. While it is fortunate for the invaders that the Spanish did not have the initiative to make greater use of sailors and naval ordnance in the first battle of the war, this is especially true of the later battles of July 1.

When Colonel Theodore Roosevelt gave up command of the Rough Riders, he stated in a farewell address to his men: "Now I want to say just a word more to some of the men I see standing around, not of your number. I refer to the colored regiments who occupied the right and left flanks at Guasimas, the Ninth and Tenth Cavalry Regiments. The Spaniards called them 'Smoked Yankees,' but we found them to be an excellent breed of Yankees."

Such a compliment to the black soldiers started an avalanche of additional praise. Many concluded that, had the black Tenth Cavalry not come up at Las Guasimas and destroyed the Spanish blockhouse and driven off the Spaniards, Roosevelt and his men would have been in serious trouble. The trap in which they were caught had a barbed wire fence on one side and a precipice on the other. Not just Captain Capron and Hamilton Fish, Jr., but the whole command would possibly have been killed or injured. The Battle of Las Guasimas was heavily fought and proved to be a victory for the Americans, but was close to being a disaster. While the battle was of short duration (two and a half hours), there were significant casualties on both sides. The victory had consequences that reached far beyond the understanding of those involved.

John J. Pershing, himself a member of the black Tenth Cavalry Regiment that had proved so effective in the battle, believed that the war was won at Las Guasimas. He later wrote: "The Spanish position was naturally very strong and the ease with which it was taken surprised our command. Without prejudice to later operations, Linares, the Spanish general commanding the Santiago district, could have brought to Las Guasimas as reinforcements, not only the sailors of Cervera's fleet, but other troops from the west of the city. The road to Santiago was the only one available to the Americans and by holding the favorable position at Las Guasimas the Spaniards could have delayed our forces there till disease drove us off."

Linares, the commander-in-chief of the Spanish troops, made a serious mistake in the extraordinarily unsound disposition of his troops, spread out in an arc to the east and north of Santiago. He should have concentrated his forces at a point where he could strongly engage the enemy advancing by either of only two roads, especially where the road from the coast crossed that narrow pass through the coastal range of mountains at Las Guasimas.

Had the enemy been successful in stopping the advance of the Americans by controlling the single road leading inland, the Americans would have been halted for an indefinite period. By holding the favorable strategic position at Las Guasimas, the Spaniards could have imprisoned them in the coastal jungles until disease destroyed their fighting ability, as actually did happen within two weeks after their arrival in Cuba. The ravages of disease would have so weakened American troops that further military action would have been impossible. One wonders at the mind-set of the Spanish high command that would ignore the very favorable defensive possibilities of Las Guasimas and order a retreat from such a strategic position. The Spanish miscalculation was another of those fortuitous elements contributing to the success of the invaders.

Details relating to a massive assault on a foreign shore are certainly easy to miss, but it is definitely unusual for an officer with the rank of general to be forgotten for any length of time. General Shafter had sent General Kent to command some transports moving westward toward the city of Cabanas in a feint to confuse the Spaniards as to exactly where the invasion would take place. The existence of General Kent, his staff, and one brigade of troops was completely overlooked for a period of three days during the excitement of the Battle of Las Guasimas and its aftermath. Finally, someone remembered the orders given him, and he was recalled.

While these events were taking place, another contingent of black soldiers was on a very dangerous mission on the southern coast of Cuba, some 160 miles to the west of Santiago. On June 21, 1898, a group of Cuban rebel soldiers that had mustered at Tampa with a detachment of the black Tenth Cavalry and white American infantrymen had succeeded in landing at a coastal town called Jucaro. There they had made contact with the Cuban insurgent army under General Maximo Gomez.

The black troops, completely isolated from American forces, fought alongside Cuban insurgents. The black cavalrymen, under Lieutenant Carter B. Johnson, participated in several notable engagements including the capture of a town called El Hebro. Their most remarkable exploit was the rescue of a group of their compatriots, white soldiers that had been surrounded by the enemy and isolated on a peninsula. Even though three rescue attempts by others had failed, a contingent of four black cavalrymen volunteered for the extremely dangerous mission and were able to land on the peninsula at night and extricate their fellow countrymen. The Medal of Honor was later awarded to each of the four black privates.

11

War stalked forth from its hiding-place . . .

—Euripides

The Battle of El Caney

With layers of hungry vultures circling overhead, the Americans hastily buried those killed in the battle at Las Guasimas and did what they could for their wounded. The black Tenth Cavalry, with the main body of the army, moved forward through the gap in the coastal range of hills at Las Guasimas into the jungled valley beyond. To the west, the San Juan Hills overlooking Santiago were easily visible some three miles away. The upper slopes of the mountain range called San Juan Hill on the west and El Caney to the north had thin vegetation, but heavy entrenchments criss-crossed the bare areas in front of the fortifications at their summits. Although all hillsides in the irregular mountain range were moderately steep, they were especially so at El Caney.

After crossing the coastal ridge, the single road leaving Las Guasimas for Santiago snakes across the valley until it reaches a hill called El Pozo. This was one of a series of isolated hills dotting the valley and the location of a former sugar refinery that had been selected by General Shafter as the site for the largest portion of the

Americans' feeble artillery. In preparation for their assault on the heights above Santiago, they camped at several sites near a small village named Sevilla, close to El Pozo. From here one could fire across the valley into enemy lines on San Juan Hill.

The black Twenty-fourth Infantry, the last regiment to land at Daiquiri, finally moved to the front about two days after the Battle of Las Guasimas. By June 30, all expeditionary forces had encamped a few miles from the northern village of El Caney where the Spaniards were busily strengthening their hilltop fortifications.

General Shafter, at three hundred pounds, made only one foray on June 30, 1898, to the top of El Pozo to inspect the topography of the planned field of battle. Thereafter, throughout the actual fighting he remained in his tent as much as possible and used it as his command headquarters for meetings with his senior officers to outline objectives and plan strategy.[21] The tropical heat later proved so extremely debilitating to the general that he often flirted with actual heat prostration. His physical problems, aggravated by an acute flareup of a painful gouty toe, were so severe that, when he did move outside, four men carried him on a barn door from place to place. From this platform he conferred with subordinates and delegated to them the choice of routes to the attack and the planning of battle tactics.

Shafter's approach to leadership was in the tradition of General Grant, who had sent his mission orders to General Sherman for the destruction of the army of General Joseph Johnston: "I do not propose to lay down for you a plan of campaign; but simply to lay down the work it is desirable to have done and leave you free to execute it in your own way." As the subsequent battle would demonstrate, his philosophy of leadership was exactly what was necessary in a heavy jungle that made communication difficult. A few years earlier, Field Marshal Helmuth von Moltke had written advice on individual initiative in warfare: "A favourable situation will never be exploited if commanders wait for orders. The highest commander and the youngest soldier must always be conscious of the fact that omission and inactivity are worse than resorting to the wrong expedient."

To General Shafter's credit, he held a strategy meeting on the night of June 30 to go over final details of preparations for the battles the following day. Unfortunately, during the short five-day interval following the Battle of Las Guasimas, fever (probably malaria) had struck down Fighting Joe Wheeler, making him too ill to attend the meeting. He sent Brigadier General Sumner to serve in his stead as commander of the cavalry division. General Wheeler was only temporarily incapacitated, however, and was present during all of the fighting on the following day, returning to full command later in the day.[22] General Young, in charge of the First Cavalry Regiment, had also fallen ill and was unable to attend, so new leaders were appointed. Colonel Leonard Wood was entrusted with leadership of the Second Cavalry Brigade and, much to his delight, Colonel Roosevelt was given command of the First Volunteer Cavalry Regiment, his own Rough Riders. Two months previously he declined to lead his troops because he felt that he had not had enough experience to be an effective leader, but he had stated at the time that after one month with his troops he was confident that he would then have the necessary competence. Thus fate again played into the hands of this extraordinary man.

Leo Tolstoy, a student of warfare and especially of the battles between Russia and Napoleon's armies, insisted that the commander-in-chief of an attacking army, regardless of what he might think, has no real control over events—after he has given the order to attack. Tolstoy stated: "The soldiers of the French Army went out to slay their fellow man at Borodino, not owing to Napoleon's commands, but through their own desire to do so." Similarly, General Shafter, having given his senior officers orders about the basic details of the battle, was no longer in control of the course of events. The abilities, determination, and enthusiasm of the officers, non-commissioned officers, and troops were to be the critical factors in the coming battle. That Shafter's control was no longer effective became evident twice on the day of the battles, when his orders to retreat were disregarded.

Shafter had stationed himself on a hill far removed from the fighting, thus adding to the problem of satisfactory communication with his officers on the battlefield. If one were to argue that the Battle of Las Guasimas was a minor skirmish, not a significant battle, one could then conclude that, in regard to land warfare, the Spanish-American War was a one-day war, both major land battles having been fought on July 1, 1898. Two separate but simultaneous battles took place on that day, and, although each had as its objective the overthrow of well-fortified hilltop entrenchments and forts, they bore little resemblance in how they were directed and fought.

So well constructed and manned were the Spanish fortifications that the numerical superiority of the attacking Americans was of little consequence. Herbert Sargent, writing about the battles a few years after the war, stressed the Spanish advantage: "It may be said without exaggeration that one soldier behind the entrenchments of El Caney or on San Juan Hill was equal in fighting power to six or eight soldiers advancing to attack him."

Shafter's plans were for a division of infantry under General Henry Lawton to capture a fort, named El Caney (most historians have called the fort El Caney, but its actual name is El Visa, with the nearby town being El Caney), situated on a strategically placed hill somewhat to the north and east of the main enemy lines on San Juan Hill. The fort, with four adjacent wooden blockhouses, was a threat to any American force attacking San Juan Hill, because its field of fire lay just to the north and east of the proposed line assaulting San Juan Hill. General Shafter therefore thought it essential to first reduce El Caney before committing troops to an attack on San Juan Hill. Intelligence reports from Cuban insurgents had reported that the fort was heavily defended. The fort was manned by no more than five or six hundred Spanish troops, but it was extremely well constructed, equipped with artillery, and well protected by three or four lines of deeply dug trenches connecting rifle pits with the blockhouses. The new defensive device, barbed wire, had been strung in front of the trenches making them even more difficult to penetrate.[23]

The contours of the steep conical hill made access to the summit extremely difficult. Particularly steep on its southern flank, the hill had a less precipitous gully to the north. While it was possible to surround the fortified summit on three sides, the fourth side to the northwest was connected by a five hundred-yard level road to the inhabited town of El Caney, where Spanish soldiers stationed in the town had a clear field of fire on any attacking Americans climbing the steep slopes to the fortifications at the summit of the hill.

Continuing their advance toward the old fort on the evening of June 30, the Americans bivouacked in the road about two miles from El Caney. As the weary Americans lay on the ground to sleep, if possible, in preparation for their rendezvous with death or injury the following day, they inevitably felt the fear and anxiety that all soldiers describe prior to entry into battle. Making rest even more difficult were the wet woolen uniforms, the humidity, and the ever present and unfamiliar jungle noises coming in choruses from tropical insects, accentuated by the occasional cry of a night-bird. Hordes of mosquitoes and flies buzzed around their faces biting whatever flesh was exposed, but even more disturbing were the large numbers of land crabs that seemed to fill the jungle around them, rustling and crackling obscenely in the night. Cuban land crabs, hideous creatures that at maturity attain a foot in width, are persistent predators in search of any food or dead flesh. As they moved around in the jungle, the loud unfamiliar noises they made in the underbrush kept nervous sentries so on edge that, from time to time during the restless night, a shouted challenge rang out, punctuated by a gunshot.

When the sky lightened at dawn, the land crabs retreated

under the soil. Loud exotic tropical birdsongs proclaimed the beginning of a fateful day. Early on the morning of July 1, word was passed along the line for all companies to fall in, with no bugle call being sounded and no coffee made. Silence was thought essential because of plans to surprise the enemy. Surprise was unlikely, however, because, on the preceding night, the valley had been dotted with conspicuous fires used for cooking the Americans' evening meals.

The importance of the Battle of El Caney has not been noted in some histories describing the Spanish-American War. Military intelligence, received from the insurgent Cubans, had informed the Americans that El Caney was defended by only about five hundred Spaniards. But this did not take into account the connecting road between the fortifications at El Visa (where the trenches were located), the stone fort, five wooden blockhouses, and the town of El Caney itself, where Spaniards had occupied homes and buildings, giving them a direct line of fire onto the western and southern sides of the steep slopes leading to the top. The town of El Caney was also connected by a well-maintained road to Santiago and the Spanish fortifications on San Juan Hill, about three miles to its west. General Lawton's timetable had allocated about an hour and a half to accomplish the Americans' first mission of the day, which was to overcome the defenders of El Caney. Lawton's troops were then to turn around, descend to the main highway and join the extreme right side of the American forces who would be just beginning their attack on the heights of San Juan Hill.

The favorable strategic disposition of the Spanish troops at

El Caney undoubtedly accounted for the unexpected difficulties encountered by sixty-six hundred American troops in overcoming the Spanish positions manned by only five hundred defenders. The defending Spanish had the advantage of freedom of movement between their trenches and blockhouses, as well as access to the resources of the town of El Caney. Adequate artillery support would have been of immeasurable help to the attacking troops, but only four field guns were available, and these fired the old-style gunpowder. Military wisdom, learned over centuries of warfare, has taught that to attack fortified heights without first giving them the full force of an artillery attack is the height of folly.

Shortly after the Americans started toward the El Caney fort at 6:30 a.m., the few pieces of American field artillery started firing and were promptly replied to by artillery fire from the enemy fort. Accurate return fire by the enemy was relatively easy because American artillery, firing from a clump of trees, created so much smoke that their position was easily located. When American artillery started firing on the blockhouse, the black Twenty-fifth Infantry had not yet reached the position from which it had planned to begin its assault. It took until the middle of the afternoon before American artillerymen could figure the proper range for their guns. When they finally did, the impending assault on the hilltop fortifications had a better chance of success.

Of the sixty-six hundred American troops assaulting the heights of El Caney, only those in the Twenty-fifth Infantry were black, constituting 15 percent of the troops attacking the hilltop.

The northern and eastern approaches to the summit were assigned to General Chaffee's brigade, composed of three infantry regiments. General Ludlow attacked the western side of the hill with a brigade of three regiments. From the south, the Twenty-fifth Infantry under Colonel Nelson Miles made its attempt to reach the crest.

When American troops had finally reached the point from which they could make an attack, the Spanish lines of entrenched soldiers still could not be seen. The only hint as to the position of the enemy was the blockhouse situated on the highest point of the steep hill. So dense was the undergrowth that a soldier could not see on a line more than fifty yards ahead. The Spaniards, however, from their elevated position in the blockhouse and trenches on the hilltop, had easily located the American forces in the bushes and opened fire upon them. As the Twenty-fifth Infantry slithered upward through the underbrush toward the hilltop, it was surprised to meet companies of the Second Massachusetts Volunteers retreating.

Men of the Second Massachusetts Volunteers had become easy targets for the Spanish because their obsolete black-powder rifles created a cloud of smoke when fired. So massive was the enemy small arms fire as a result of the telltale smoke, the American volunteers had been ordered to retire, although their absence further reduced the attacking forces (and increased the proportion of black troops involved). The volunteers seemed completely whipped; they took the occasion to warn the advancing troops that there was no use to advance farther because they would be running into certain death, with one of them declaring:

"You can't see a thing and they are slaughtering our men."

For the assault on the southern slope of the hill, Colonel Daggett of the black Twenty-fifth Infantry placed two companies in the firing line and held two other companies in support. Held in reserve were the four remaining companies, one of which was commanded by Captain Walter S. Scott. Heavy enemy fire pelted the forward contingent of American troops as they crawled up the hill, squirming through the underbrush and across small open fields in the face of incessant fire. Small groups of soldiers scuttled madly across the fields and plopped heavily down into the dirt after only five or six yards of running forward and fired blindly at the fort. By about one o'clock in the afternoon, the last of the supporting companies of the Twenty-fifth Infantry had moved into position on the attacking line. Augmenting the heavy enemy rifle and artillery fire from the fort was a withering fire from the town of El Caney on their left. To counter the intense flanking fire from the town, a detachment of soldiers was sent to the west.

Near 1:30 p.m., when the attack had been going on for some four or five hours with little evidence of progress, General Shafter sent General Lawton an order to break off the engagement, withdraw his troops, and reassemble them for a move westward to assist Generals Kent and Sumner at the base of San Juan Hill. Providentially, General Lawton disregarded the order of his superior officer and decided to press the action even more vigorously than before.[24]

After many hours of fruitless effort, the feeble American artillery finally found its range at a crucial time and began knocking down chunks from the walls of the stone fort. Nevertheless, it was clear that little progress had been made after five hours of frontal assault on the Spanish fortifications. Officers of the Twenty-fifth Infantry then ordered sharpshooters to direct their fire solely at the openings of the building to slow the Spanish fire.

After so many hours of taking withering small arms fire from the Spanish and with little progress to show for it, the Twenty-fifth Infantry, led by an excited master sergeant, leapt from the underbrush and suddenly started charging up the hill with the howl of steel fragments tearing apart the air just overhead. Once again the black soldiers screamed loud Comanche Indian war cries as they attacked, creating an eerie atmosphere and certain fear in the hearts of the Spanish.

There is uncertainty as to who started the charge, but one thing was certain: at the time it was made, excitement was running high and each man was his own captain, fighting accordingly. The Fourth United States Infantry, fighting to the left of the Twenty-fifth Infantry, hesitated briefly when the black troops rushed up the hill shouting war whoops. On the right flank of the Twenty-fifth Infantry, the Twelfth Infantry advanced up the eastern slope of the hill accompanied by a journalist who later shared his thoughts in *Harper's*: "The left side of the Twelfth I noticed was closing in, apparently for a charge, which in fact went forward with a cheer at once. The fort was carried at 3:30 p.m., but the fight was not over. To that point it had taken nine hours of steady fighting."

A famous fighting man from a later era, General George C. Patton, believed, "No sane man is unafraid in battle, but discipline produces in him a form of vicarious courage." Such seemed to be the case with the attacking American soldiers as they emerged from the covering underbrush and advanced, seemingly oblivious to the perfect hailstorm of bullets, the spang of lead smashing into rocks, the blazing sun and the barbed wire entanglements as they charged the blockhouse. Continuing to move up in spite of heavy fire, they soon saw a white flag sticking out of the window of the fort in a sign of surrender. The Spaniard holding the flag was felled by a bullet, but another took his place. At this point the firing stopped. The Twenty-fifth Infantry entered the fort.

12

If it be a sin to covet honor . . .

—Shakespeare, *King Henry V*

Mixed Credits

Senator Hiram Johnson of California stated in a 1917 Senate speech: "In war, truth is the first casualty." Much controversy arose over which outfit was first to arrive at the fort of El Caney, with Major General Chaffee claiming the white Twelfth Infantry had taken the fort and that the black Twenty-fifth Infantry, keeping its fire aimed at the village, had arrived later. Opposing this claim was Colonel Daggett, commander of the Twenty-fifth Infantry, who requested that the official documents be changed to reflect testimony of those who had been in the battle. He demanded that those officers present submit separate official reports.

That a white American was in the fort when the black soldiers arrived seems certain. He proved to be a Hearst war correspondent, James Creelman, who was shortly thereafter shot through the shoulder while recovering the Spanish flag.[25] George Kennan, another correspondent in Cuba, stated that Creelman had somehow arrived at the fort ahead of the troops. On the left side of the firing line was a slight gully up which one could move close to the fort. Apparently, as soon as the Spanish officers had left and before members of the American infantry had advanced to the fort, Creelman had climbed up the gully and slipped into the back of the building. Probably it was he who ordered a black trooper of the Twenty-fifth Infantry, Private Butler, to turn over to him the Spanish flag that the soldier had retrieved from the fleeing Spanish. Thinking Creelman was a military man, since he was "dressed something like an officer," Private Butler gave him the flag. Before giving it to him, however, he tore off a corner in order later to be able to show that he had actually had the flag in his possession.

Creelman's version of how he obtained the flag is quoted in *The Correspondents' War*: "Suddenly I thought of the flag. It was the thing I had come to get. I wanted it for the *Journal*. The *Journal* had provoked the war, and it was only fair that the *Journal* should have the first flag captured in the greatest land battle of the war. I looked up at the flagstaff and found that the flag was not there. I rushed up to the Spanish officer and demanded the flag. He shrugged his shoulders and told me that a bomb had just carried it away. I was in terror lest someone else get the precious emblem of victory first, so I hurried out of the door to the verge of the hill, and there lay the red and yellow banner in the dust still fastened to the top of the shattered flagstaff."

Later that day, while William Randolph Hearst was inspecting the site of the heroic battle, he found his employee, the wounded Creelman, lying along the side of the road. Ever the newspaper reporter, Hearst interviewed the wounded man and wrote down his comments in spite of Spanish bullets flying overhead.

Hearst later interviewed Colonel Laine, a correspondent familiar with the rebel forces, and learned that after the Battle of El Caney the Americans had turned over their Spanish prisoners to the Cuban rebels. The rebels had then decapitated the forty prisoners of war. Evidently because he was sympathetic with the rebel cause, Mr. Hearst did not report this gruesome atrocity in his newspapers; however, such butchery would have made screaming headlines had the Spanish been guilty of the act, or had a true journalistic professionalism influenced the conscience of Hearst.[26]

Eight weeks following the Battle of El Caney, Major General Chaffee wrote a letter to the headquarters of the Second Division of the Fifth Army Corps, stating in part, "It is not disputed, however, some of the Twenty-fifth fired on the stone fort. The troops arriving at the stone fort were there in the following order: Twelfth Infantry, which took the place; the command of General Bates some minutes later; the Twenty-fifth Infantry. A captain of the Twenty-fifth Infantry claimed the capture of the place from me at the same time and on the battlefield, and I told him then his proposition was absurd, and stated to him the order in which the troops arrived."[27]

So much controversy about credit for actually taking the fort brought forth an August 22 letter from Colonel Daggett:

> I have the honor to submit a supplementary report to the original made on the 19th of July, 1898, of the Battle of El Caney de Cuba, so far as related to the part taken therein by the Twenty-fifth Infantry.
>
> (1) I stated in the original report that the Twenty-fifth Infantry,

in advancing, broke away from and left the Fourth Infantry behind. This may inferentially reflect on the latter regiment. It was not so intended, and a subsequent visit to the battlefield convinces me that it would have been impossible for that regiment to advance to the fort, and although it might have advanced a short distance farther, it would have resulted in useless slaughter, and that the battalion commander exercised excellent judgment in remaining where he did, and by his fire aiding the Twenty-fifth Infantry in its advance.

(2) Colonel Miles, then brigade commander, informed me that his first report of the battle would be brief and that a later and full report would be made. In his former report I think he failed to give credit to myself and regiment. As he was soon after relieved of the command of the brigade, I assume that no further report will be made (by Colonel Miles).

I have reported what the regiment did, but said nothing about my own action. I must, therefore, report it myself, or let it go unrecorded. Distasteful as it is to me, I deem it my duty to my children to state the facts and my claims based thereon as follows:

(1) I was ordered to put two companies on the firing line. Before this line advanced, the brigade commander informed me and personal examination verified that my right was in the air and exposed. On my own judgment I ordered a company, as flankers, to that part of the line.

(2) As soon as the line had rested and become steadied at its first halt, I ordered it to advance, and it continued to advance, although it broke away from the rest of the brigade.

(3) As this exposed the left to a galling and dangerous fire, I ordered, on my own judgment, a company to reinforce that part of the line, and a company from the regimental reserve also to the fighting line.

(4) These are facts, and as my orders were to keep my left joined to the right of the Fourth Infantry, and received no further orders, my claims are as follows:

(1) That it was necessary to place a company on the right as flankers.

(2) That the conditions offered an opportunity to advance after the first halt and I took advantage of it.

(3) That the left being exposed by this advance of the line beyond the rest of the brigade, it was proper and necessary to reinforce it by two companies.

(4) That the two companies first deployed could not have reached the stone fort.

(5) That the three companies added to the firing line gave it the power to reach the fort.

(6) That the advance beyond the rest of the brigade was a bold and, without support, dangerous movement, but that the result justified the act. Had it failed I would have been held responsible.

(7) That I saw at each stage of the battle what ought to be done and did it. Results show that it was done at the right moment.

(8) That the Twenty-fifth Infantry caused the surrender of the stone fort.

I desire to repeat that it is with great reluctance that I make so much of this report as relates to myself, and nothing but a sense of duty would impel me to do it.

A letter written by First Lieutenant French of the Twenty-fifth Infantry stated that his battalion, under Captain Walter S. Scott, "had arrived about one o'clock in the afternoon at a point about eight-hundred yards to the south and east of the Fort. This had been designated as the attacking line. Presently, after advancing a few yards, we were subjected to a galling fire from the stone fort, the trenches in its front and a blockhouse on its right. The line steadily moved forward, directing its fire at the stone fort and the trenches surrounding it. When within about 150 yards from the Fort, the line was halted, and several sharpshooters were ordered by their company officers to fire at the loopholes. Finally, when the men had regained their wind, a rush was made, part of the line going through a cornfield. At the foot, the line was again halted and, after a few moments rest, charged up the hill and the fort surrendered." Lieutenant French said that he went into the fort and captured a Spanish lieutenant and several enlisted men, whom he handed over to an officer of the Twelfth Infantry. Testimony of other officers was similar, confirming that the Twenty-fifth Infantry had directed its fire at the fort and was largely responsible for capturing the fort.

The letter of Colonel Daggett contains the information as to which troops were under Captain Walter S. Scott, something that extensive research had not heretofore presented to me. Colonel Daggett also stated, in a letter written immediately following the battle, that the regiment of the Twenty-fifth Infantry formed a firing line on the right of the Fourth Infantry and was facing the Spanish fort, a blockhouse about a mile distant. On moving forward, the battalion, composed of Companies C, D, E, G, H and commanded by Captain Scott, received the fire of the enemy. After advancing about four hundred yards, it was then subjected to a galling fire on its left. Once they found cover, the company officers skillfully led the battalion on a rapid advance up the hill to the fort. Colonel Daggett further related: "On arriving a short distance from the fort, the white flag was waved to our companies, but a cross-fire prevented the enemy from advancing with it, or our officers from receiving it." Daggett continued: "About twenty minutes later a battalion of some other regiment advanced to the rear of the fort, completely protected from enemy fire by favorable topography, and received the flag, but the men of the Twenty-fifth Infantry entered the fort at the same time. All the men and officers behaved gallantly. One officer was killed and three were wounded, with eight enlisted men killed and twenty wounded. In the firing line were about two hundred men and ten officers. The small losses were attributed to the bravery and skill of the company officers."

Because there was so much controversy about Major General Chaffee's comment that the Twenty-fifth Infantry had not fired at the fort, there were other supporting letters. Lieutenant Caldwell of the Twenty-fifth Infantry wrote a letter certifying that the company he commanded, Company H of the Twenty-fifth Infantry, directed its fire almost exclusively on the stone fort and the trench a few yards from its base. He said that very little of the company's fire was directed on the town, and none of it before the fort was carried.

Lieutenant James A. Moss, of the Twenty-fifth Infantry, wrote that, from about one o'clock in the afternoon until the time of capture of El Caney, he had been in command of two companies that formed part of the Twenty-fifth Infantry firing line. From about 2:55 p.m. until the capture of the town, almost the entire Twenty-fifth Infantry firing line had been under his observation. He concluded that from that time until about half an hour later the fire of the entire Twenty-fifth Infantry was directed against the fort. He also stated that, during this period of battle, the Twenty-fifth Infantry firing line was about 150 yards from the stone fort. From the time the firing line began firing until the surrender of the fort (about two to three hours later), he observed the companies under his command and had all others within his view. From this he concluded that the fire of the entire Twenty-fifth Infantry was against the fort. Moss further stated that, at about 3:20 p.m., he was standing about 150 yards from the fort when he plainly saw a Spaniard appear in the door of the fort. For two or three seconds, before he was shot, the Spaniard waved a white flag at the Twenty-fifth Infantry line. Another Spaniard picked up the flag and also waved it at the Twenty-fifth Infantry firing line. With the white flag having been twice presented to the Twenty-fifth Infantry firing line, and all fire from the stone fort having ceased, the firing line rushed forward and entered the fort. Turning toward the town, they then poured a vigorous fire on the small blockhouse and the town of El Caney.

Who first arrived at the Spanish fort and who first took possession of the enemy's battle flag has been lost in the kaleidoscope of history, but the valor exhibited by those who captured the well-defended fort should be long remembered. Black troops, heavily involved in the battle, apparently were the first to begin the charge up the hill to the fort, and their numbers, combined with their bravery and heedless attitude toward death, were fundamental to victory, an outcome that surprised even General Shafter, who had earlier ordered General Lawton to withdraw his troops from the attack on the hilltop.

Later, writing about the battle, a black sergeant noted with pride that the "coolness and bravery that had characterized the black soldiers' fathers in the sixties, when they participated in the Civil War, had been handed down to their sons of the nineties." He stated: "If anyone doubted the fitness of the colored soldier for active field duty, he should contact the white commanders who had witnessed their performance at the 'hornets nest.'"

Stephen Bonsal, a reporter who reported vividly on the battles of these few days, summed up his assessment of black soldiers: "The orders given to the colored regiments brought them well to the front in the different divisions to which they were assigned, and their courage and soldierly efficiency kept them there. They may have been, they certainly were, favored by the fortunes of war, but in the sequel they showed that they were worthy to receive such favors. The Twenty-fifth fought at El Caney under Lawton, and shared with the white men of the Twelfth Infantry the honor and the losses incident to capturing the old stone fort. This was the key to their position, and the Spaniards defended it with a stubborn valor that moved all observers in admiration. Indeed, the defense and capture of this fort have often been characterized as the most striking exploit of the campaign."

One of the captured Spanish officers accused the Americans of taking unfair advantage of them by using black troops who fought so ferociously. "Why," he complained, "even your Negroes fight better than any troops I ever saw."

Since the enemy still held the village of El Caney, where it had fortified positions, it took more fighting to capture the village. So heavy was the defensive fire from the town that two more hours of fighting were necessary before the Spaniards abandoned their positions in the village and retreated toward Santiago. The battle ended at about five o'clock in the afternoon after ten hours of fighting. This was at least an hour after the end of the Battle of San Juan Hill that had taken place simultaneously on the opposite side of the valley.

One commentator spoke of the Battle of El Caney in more detail: "The charge at El Caney has been little spoken of, but it was quite as great a show of bravery as the famous taking of San Juan Hill. A word more in regard to the charge up the hill. It was not the glorious run from the edge of some nearby picket to the top of a small hill, as many may imagine. This particular charge was a tough, hard climb, over rising ground which, were a man in perfect physical shape, he would climb slowly. Part of the charge was made over soft, plowed land, a part through a lot of prickly pineapple plants and barbed wire entanglements. It was slow, hard work under a blazing July sun and a perfect hailstorm of bullets, which, thanks to the poor marksmanship of the Spaniards, went high. It has been generally admitted by all fair-minded writers that the colored soldiers saved the day both at El Caney and at San Juan Hill. They had accomplished something which orthodox military strategists had always considered well nigh impossible, namely, the attack and capture of a high redoubt, over open ground, with fewer weapons of poorer quality than those of a heavily entrenched foe."

Of the sixty-six hundred troops assaulting the heights of El Caney, the black Twenty-fifth Infantry comprised some 15 percent of the total. The black soldiers lost 25 percent of the officers killed in the battle and about 13 percent of all officers who were wounded, while death and injury among black soldiers was around 10 percent of total casualties. These figures support the position that black soldiers were deeply involved both in this battle and, as will be noted by other casualty figures, in the battle taking place simultaneously on San Juan Hill.

The physical endurance of General Lawton's troops knew no bounds. After burying their dead at sunset, they set off to the west down the road through El Caney in the direction of San Juan Hill, hoping to take a short-cut to quickly reinforce the precarious American position on that newly captured ridge. The men had slept only four hours the preceding night and had spent some ten hours fighting with nothing to eat, and they were especially fatigued from having climbed the steep approaches to attack the fortifications at the top of the hill at El Caney.

Because they encountered some Spanish pickets on the much shorter and more direct road to the San Juan ridge, the commanding officer decided to turn the troops around, go back through El Caney, and take the jungle road through the valley used earlier by the forces attacking San Juan Hill. After a brief rest at the site of the American artillery battery at El Pozo, they continued to march west. It was not until noon the next day that they finally took their position on the northernmost end of the American line, only a short distance from El Caney from where they had started their circuitous march. With their deployment being nearest the enemy, they were immediately put to work digging trenches, using bayonets for picks and hands for shovels. When completed, the trenches were immediately occupied by white troops, while the blacks continued their excavations elsewhere.

General Lawton was often heard to tell a story about the march of the black troops from El Caney: "The night of the El Caney affair, when my division was marching back to El Pozo to take up a new position the next morning, I was sitting with Major

G. Creighton Webb, inspector-general of my staff and one of the pluckiest men I know, at the side of the road. My men were filing past, and we watched them. They were tired out but full of ginger. The day was just beginning to dawn when we heard someone coming down the road, talking at the top of their lungs. He talked and laughed and laughed and talked, and the men with him were chattering and joking.

"'Here come the colored troops,' said Webb, and sure enough the Twenty-fifth Infantry came along. The man who was doing the talking was a six-foot corporal; he carried two guns and two cartridge belts loaded full, and the man to whom the extra gun belt belonged was limping along beside him. The tall corporal was further weighted down with his blankets and haversack, but in his arms he carried a dog, the mascot of his company.

"'Here, corporal,' said Webb, 'didn't you march all last night?'

"'Yes, sir,' said the corporal, trying to salute.

"'And didn't you fight all day?'

"'Sure, sir.'

"'And haven't you been marching since ten o'clock tonight?"

"'Yes, sir,' said the corporal.

"'Well then,' shouted Webb, 'What in thunder are you carrying that dog for?'

"'Why boss, the dog's tired' was the reply.

"Webb just rolled over in the dirt and laughed and cried like a boy."

Since the formation of black cavalry and infantry units

several years after the Civil War, it had been customary for officers to use black soldiers, before or after the fighting, to perform the most menial tasks, such as stringing wire, constructing roads, preparing the railbeds for the expanding railroads, and digging trenches when necessary. The practice continued until segregation of all troops was finally ended after World War II.[28]

One assumes that officers, in order to lead effectively, must have an affection for the troops under their command. It follows that this was true of those officers leading black regiments. As the assignment of lack soldiers to the most difficult of menial jobs had been the practice for many decades, it is logical to assume that this practice eventually aroused misgivings and feelings of guilt in the minds of those in command—after achieving victory under fire, the black soldiers were then made to do the degrading tasks of others who had not been under fire. This unfair treatment must have been clearly evident and is certain to have created bitterness within the hearts of many good men.

One thing is certain, however; eleven days after the battles of San Juan and El Caney, during which interval they had done nothing but dig trenches, soldiers of the Twenty-fifth Infantry must have felt they had done more than their share of grubbing in the soil.

13

Seeking the bubble reputation even in
the cannon's mouth . . .

—Shakespeare, *As You Like It*

The Battle of San Juan Hill

During the day-long engagement at El Caney (an engagement planned to take, at the most, only two or three hours) the
other three black units, the Twenty-fourth Infantry and the
Ninth and Tenth cavalries, were simultaneously assaulting the
Spanish entrenchments atop San Juan Hill. While it did not
become evident until several days later, the two battles of July 1,
1898, were the turning point in the war and culminated in
American victory over the Spanish.

Although it had not been General Shafter's original plan
(Shafter had planned to assault the fortifications at San Juan Hill
on July 2, after his troops had been deployed at the base of the hill
on July 1), the two battles occurred simultaneously on July 1,
with victory hanging in the balance throughout the day. After
many hours of extremely difficult fighting, the score was finally
settled in favor of the Americans. Lacking artillery of any consequence, the foot soldiers successfully shouldered the burden of

reducing heavily fortified blockhouses and forts on the summits of steep hills protected by trenches secured by many heavy strands of barbed wire, an obstacle which they were able to surmount in spite of the absence of wire cutters, which had never been unloaded from the invasion ships.

After crossing the coastal range and climbing to the pass at Las Guasimas, the road to Santiago then descends into a three-mile wide valley whose western boundary is a series of lofty ridges overlooking Santiago farther to the west. These ridges are known collectively as San Juan Hill, with a number of peaks and crests named individually. The road crossing the valley itself was in miserable condition, so narrow in places that two wagons could not pass, and just wide enough in other places for only four men to walk abreast. The sides of the road consisted of a solid wall of impenetrable jungle. During the days leading up to July 1st, late afternoon deluges had turned the road into a quagmire and had caused flooding of small streams and two rivers that crossed the valley floor just at the beginning of the slope up San Juan Hill.

Shafter expected to have his entire attacking force travel down the rutted, muddy, narrow road, the only approach to the enemy's positions on the distant hill. Complicating the exiting of the troops from the jungle road was the presence of the San Juan River, which, although shallow, lay at the edge of the jungle very close to the Spanish lines. At the base of San Juan Hill the First Infantry Division was to deploy to the left of the road and encircle the southern approaches to the Spanish fortifications, and the unmounted cavalry division was to fan out to the right of the road and cover the eastern flank of the hill. When the deployment had been completed, all troops were to await orders before advancing up the hill in whatever fashion they chose to take the fortifications on its summit.

On July 1, following a brief early morning artillery exchange, American troops moved down the narrow, rutted road toward their destiny. Progress proved to be extremely slow due to troop congestion and the heavy mud.

Although the infantry moved out first, within a short time word was passed down the line for them to form a line of twos in order to permit cavalry soldiers to reach their assigned sectors at about the same time as the infantry. Thus, a column with four soldiers abreast, two infantrymen and two cavalrymen, like steers moving down a cattle chute, advanced through the dank tunnel created by the overhanging jungle that narrowed to a choke point at the river crossing. Here the road became almost impassable and caused the entire column to move even more slowly.

The most congested portion of the road, where men and materiel were backed up and struggling to advance, was the site of a most interesting episode, courtesy of the Signal Corps. The Signal Corps had brought an observation balloon from the States, and, with much difficulty, had dragged it down the road toward Santiago. Such balloons had proven of some value in the Civil War. The memorable balloon, after being tugged along the trail by its attendants, was then filled with hydrogen and sent aloft in the midst of the chaos and confusion resulting from the impasse on the congested road.

Colonel Derby and Major John Maxwell were in its basket, using their elevated position to survey the battlefield and its approaches. Fortunately for the Americans' timetable, the balloonists located a hitherto unknown trail leading to the left toward the open meadow at the southern base of the San Juan ridges. Leaning out of his basket, Colonel Derby called to the troops below and asked for an officer to whom he could transmit his information. General Kent immediately put the valuable information to use in order to untangle his men from the struggling melee on the road and to lead them down the newly discovered trail to their assigned area on the southern approaches to the targeted hill.

In spite of the success of the innovative bit of aerial reconnaissance, the balloon proved to be a disaster for those troops trapped on the trail beneath it because the enemy used it as a marker for the exact location of the attacking forces, giving enemy artillery an excellent target on which to fix their sights. Obscured by the jungle surrounding them, the Americans' exact location had not been precisely known by the Spanish defenders until the balloon clearly marked the location of the trail. A curtain of bullets and artillery shells struck both the balloon and the troops beneath, causing some injuries and a few deaths. Finally, the balloon was so badly torn by enemy fire that it gracefully floated to the ground with no injury to its brave occupants.[29]

The Seventy-first New York Volunteer Infantry did not distinguish itself in the Battle of San Juan Hill. Unfortunately for the fledgling volunteer soldiers, they were in the lead of the column moving down the trail that had been discovered by the observation balloon. The New York unit's soldiers had never before been under hostile fire. Three hundred of them were said never to have fired a rifle prior to enlisting. The governor of New York had refused to accept black volunteers, explaining that the color line had traditionally been enforced in New York's state militia.

When the raw recruits emerged from the shelter of the jungle, they moved out into the open in the teeth of withering fire from the Spanish on the summit of the hill above them. Never having heard the sound of enemy fire nor the crunch of a bullet striking solid flesh, they retreated into the woods from which they had just emerged. The New York militia was then ordered to stand aside to permit the rest of the regular infantry division, including the black Twenty-fourth Infantry, to pass through them in order to reach their assault position on the southern base of the hill. As veterans of the Indian Wars, the bulk of the regular infantry were hardened troops and had been under fire many times. They disdainfully skirted the volunteers cowering fearfully in the bushes and deployed on the southern slope.

It was on this trail that Colonel Liscum of the black Twenty-fourth Infantry encountered his old friend General Kent, whose division was advancing toward the southern slope of San Juan Hill. General Kent was standing in a fork in the trail with tears streaming down his cheeks, begging and pleading with the frightened soldiers of the white Seventy-first New York Volunteers: "for the love of country, liberty, honor and dignity; in the name of freedom, in the name of God; for the sake of dear mothers and fathers, to stand up like men and fight, and go to the front." His entreaties were in vain, and the new recruits fled like chickens being chased by foxes.[30]

There were striking differences between the battles of El Caney and San Juan Hill. While both battles resulted in victory for the Americans, the methods by which each victory was achieved illustrate how varied are the means to military success.

Officer leadership became seriously impaired in the assault on San Juan Hill since some 50 percent of the officers were killed or wounded a few others were said to have sat out the hottest part of the battle. Troop deployment and the attack in the Battle of San Juan Hill were, as a result, carried out primarily by small battle units (individuals, squads, or platoons).

At El Caney, the attacking troops were deployed according to orthodox Army doctrine in a standard firing line with other troops deployed on each flank to protect the assault forces. Still other companies were held in support of those on the firing line, and a third contingent was held in reserve. Very much in evidence at all times were the officers, who joined and directed the troops in their charge on the fort.

Chaos best describes the state of affairs faced by the army forces preparing for the assault on San Juan Hill. There were no great masses of soldiers charging with waving flags and no sword-pointing officers in the lead, those things one associates with the great battles of history prior to the modern era. It was the initiative and determination of each individual or small unit that ultimately drove this battle to conclusion.[31]

Among the difficulties in the terrain was the confluence of the Aguadores and San Juan rivers at a point precisely in the middle of the area where the troops were to deploy to the north and to the south when emerging from the jungle. The extraordinarily difficult terrain and the almost impassable road leading to the base of the hill contributed to the chaos. Heavy jungle covered the trail until it suddenly emerged into the open, just at the base of the hill where the rivers joined. At that point, the confusion was so great that squads, platoons, and companies lost contact with their commanding officers. Many had no clue as to the location of their regiments. As officers were killed or wounded, non-commissioned officers (sergeants or corporals, black or white) took over leadership of an intact unit until a commissioned officer could be found. If one was not found, he continued to lead until the battle was over.

It was necessary for the attacking troops, under heavy, shattering, continuous fire from above, to squeeze through the narrow point where the road crossed the San Juan River. A succession of unattached squads and companies hurried toward the hilltop, pausing to shoot and rush on again. In such confusion, the response of the troops was in accord with the later thinking of General Sir Ian Hamilton in 1921: "Let each little group understand the common objective. Then leave them to the promptings of their own consciences of what is right, rather than to the dread of doing wrong." The result was a combination of infantry and cavalry units, both white and black soldiers, fused into a mob of attacking forces, with no troops being held in reserve for reinforcement. Confusion reigned, but the objectives of the assault remained fixed in the minds of the brave soldiers subjected to continuous, harrowing fire from Spanish artillery and small arms.

When the American forces had finally extricated themselves

from the entanglements of the jungle and the threat of drowning in the river, the cavalry division occupied its assigned position on the north of the road. As had been planned, the infantry deployed to the south of the road where they discovered a comparatively unobstructed field in front of them leading to the base of the slope, up which they were to make their assault. Several heavy barbed wire entanglements at the base of the hill proved to be the only real obstruction; moreover, these defenses were difficult to bypass because most of the wire had been attached to the trunks of cut trees that were difficult to uproot.

In the storm of lead that raked the mountainside, the soldiers uprooted the posts to which loose segments of the wire had been attached. Throughout the entire advance up the hillside a murderous barrage of small arms and artillery fire came from the Spanish on the upper hillside and summit. The Thirteenth Infantry, stationed to the far left of the attacking line, had its leadership change three times within a short period because each succeeding officer was injured or killed.

John J. Pershing, a member of the officer corps of the black Tenth Cavalry Regiment, described the action as follows: "It was a hot fight—the converging artillery and infantry fire made life worth nothing. We waded the river to our armpits and formed line in an opening in dense undergrowth facing our objective, the San Juan blockhouse, all the while exposed to volley firing from front, left front, and left flank, and you know what it means to be uncertain as to the position of the enemy."[32]

The logistics related to six thousand men moving four abreast down a single trail is intriguing when one considers the problems posed by the heavy enemy gunfire at the point of exit. It seems almost impossible that men in groups of four could emerge from the jungle in a short enough interval to amass enough manpower to constitute anything like an adequate attacking force. If each group of four men squeezed out of the jungle trail every ten seconds, only twenty-four could exit each minute and no more than 1,440 each hour; so four hours were necessary for the entire attacking force to simply get out of the jungle and deploy itself.

This bottleneck effect caused the attack to be late, an attack from which there could be no retreat. One cannot fail to be impressed by the courage of the American soldiers emerging from the relative seclusion and safety of the tunnel trail in the jungle to enter the almost treeless open space at the river's edge where the base of San Juan Hill was inundated with small arms fire and shrapnel that were cutting down men as they tried to find cover in the underbrush.[33]

Tolstoy's reflections about the uselessness of a detailed battle plan apply to the assault on San Juan Hill. Colonel Roosevelt found himself in charge of not only the main body of his Rough Riders, but an equal or greater number of the black Tenth Cavalry and some of the regular First Cavalry Regiment. On getting separated from Roosevelt's regiment, some squads and platoons of the Rough Riders attached themselves to a mixture of cavalry troops to their left, led by General Sumner; however, in spite of the confusion, most squads and platoons still remained intact units. At the base of San Juan Hill the advance of the Tenth Cavalry was slowed by a powerful barrage of Spanish shells and bullets just as it arrived at the banks of the San Juan River. Spanish infantry and artillery fired from three blockhouses and from a series of entrenchments in front and to the left of the attackers. So intense was the fire that it sent the black cavalrymen sprawling in the sand, digging in for their lives with their elbows and gun butts.

The cavalry division emerged from the jungle to be met by an unexpected problem in the form of a small hill in front of the base of San Juan Hill. The summit of the hill (called "Kettle Hill" due to the presence of a large kettle for boiling molasses) was well fortified and manned by an advance skirmish line of Spanish soldiers. When Colonel Roosevelt saw the hill in front of him, he realized that he must overcome the Spanish forces occupying its summit before his primary objective could be attacked. Not to be deterred by the unexpected discovery of a well-fortified Spanish outpost, Roosevelt decided to attack it at once; officers of both the First Cavalry and the Ninth Cavalry had made similar decisions. Obstructed by two barbed wire fences, the attack was slowed until the fence posts had been pulled up, allowing the troops to advance up the steep incline under continuous fire from the Spanish situated both on San Juan Hill and the top of Kettle Hill. Roosevelt, astride his favorite horse, "Little Texas," had been able to penetrate the first barbed wire entanglement, but, on reaching the second, had to abandon his steed and continue on foot.

Simultaneous with Roosevelt's charge was a similar attack on the southern face of Kettle Hill, causing the Spanish defenders to retreat down the western slope and cross a small valley to the west to rejoin their comrades on San Juan Hill. (Since they had approached and ascended its southern side, the black Ninth Cavalry later claimed to be the first on the hill, but their claim remains disputed by the black Tenth Cavalry, the First Cavalry, and the First Volunteer Cavalry). The summit of Kettle Hill was completely exposed to enemy fire from above, delivered in thunderous volleys from Spanish rifles, machine guns and artillery. One can be certain that the large cast iron kettle on the hilltop made quite a noise when struck by missiles flying at random. Exhausted American troops were gradually reformed into semicohesive units on the hilltop, where enemy fire caused even more casualties than those sustained in the charge up the hill. Under fire was an aggregation of troops of the black Tenth Cavalry and most of the Rough Riders, some of whom, choosing not to make that dangerous charge up the hill, had drifted off to the south to join the regular cavalry brigade of General Sumner.

In his exploits of that day, Roosevelt was accompanied by a friend—newspaper reporter Richard Harding Davis. Armed with a pistol, Davis wore his usual civilian outfit of a sack suit, sun helmet with a scarf around it (a Hindu "puggaree"), and tramping boots. He participated in the charge up San Juan Hill, later declaring: "The Negro soldiers established themselves as fighting men in that engagement." Never having led troops before, Colonel Roosevelt wrestled with his inexperience. Interesting yet tragic evidence of this was his decision to advance from Kettle Hill into the little valley beyond in preparation for the ascent up the larger San Juan Hill. Failing to communicate his attack plans to his troops, he jumped over a barbed wire fence and shouted for men to follow him. After he had advanced some hundred yards down the hill, he looked back and realized that he was accompanied by only five men! Leaving these five (two of whom were killed before he returned), he rejoined his troops and rounded up the rest of the regiment, who apologized for not having heard his initial orders to charge.[34]

After having driven the Spaniards from Kettle Hill, Roosevelt noticed that General Kent's division, far to his left on the southern slopes of San Juan Hill, was beginning its upward surge toward the summit fortifications situated on the southern end of the hill. By one o'clock, Roosevelt had become acutely aware that the attack in his sector of the battle line was already three hours behind schedule due to the difficulty in advancing down the jungle trail and the unexpected presence of Kettle Hill. He summoned his three or four hundred Rough Riders, a large contingent of the black Tenth Cavalry, and a varied collection of regular soldiers from other regiments, who understood that they were to advance up the hill in whatever manner possible. Just before the charge up San Juan Hill by the Tenth Cavalry and the Rough Riders, one foreign attache, an Englishman, was heard to say that he did not see how the blockhouse was to be reached without the aid of cannon; but, after the feat was accomplished, a black soldier said: "We showed him how."[35]

A soldier interviewed after the battle had a comment about the black troops at San Juan Hill: "Before El Caney was taken, the Spaniards were on the heights of San Juan with heavy guns. All along our line an assault was made and the enemy was holding us off with terrible effect. From their blockhouse on the hill came a magazine of shot. Shrapnel shells fell in our ranks doing great damage and something had to be done or the day would have been lost. The black Ninth Cavalry and part of the black Tenth Cavalry moved across into a thicket nearby and the Spaniards rained shot upon them. They collected themselves and, like a flash, swept across the plains and charged up the hill. The enemy's guns were used with deadly effect. On and on the cavalrymen went, charging with the fury of madness. And the odd thing about it all is that these wounded heroes never will admit that they did anything out of the common. They will talk all night about those 'other fellows' but they don't about themselves, and were immensely surprised when such a fuss was made over them on their arrival and since. They simply believed they had a duty to perform and performed it."[36]

On the southern flank of the hill the black Twenty-fourth Infantry was simultaneously beginning its dramatic charge. Both General Kent of the the First Infantry Division and General Sumner of the cavalry division were acutely aware that Shafter had not planned for their division to attack the summit of the hill on July 1. Shafter and his staff had concluded that, on July 1, the attacking troops should cross the valley and deploy at the base of the hill. After being joined by General Lawton's troops following their reduction of the fort at El Caney on July 1, the entire attacking army would then be in position to launch its attack on July 2.

However, their troops had become so heavily engaged after leaving the jungle cover that it was necessary to attack rather than retreat. On the southern slope, General Kent's subordinate, General Hawkins, could not find his superior (who was involved in trying to motivate the New York volunteers) and realized that his two exposed regiments no longer could endure the brutal Spanish fusillade; so, without orders from his commanding officer, he ordered his troops to attack.

A trusted aide-de-camp of General Shafter, Lieutenant Colonel John D. Miley had accompanied the attacking troops to the base of San Juan Hill. He had left the command post at General Shafter's tent, far in the rear, to coordinate operations in the area of the attack. From reports of the battle, it is clear that one of the officers present was heard to give the order to attack. Lieutenant Colonel Miley had correctly assumed that he was the surrogate of his immediate superior, General Shafter, and therefore had the authority to order an advance if he felt it necessary. After consultation with General Sumner, on his own responsibility, he ordered the charge up San Juan Hill.

Roosevelt's attacking force suddenly broke for the base of San Juan Hill as if moved by a spontaneous impulse and slowly but implacably advanced up the incline, moving forward by degrees in spite of withering fire from above. To observers from the command post behind, the line looked very weak and thin, but eventually it proved equal to the task. It should be remembered that the attacking line had no support troops behind them, and no forces were being held in reserve to add increased strength and momentum to the assault.

Fortunately for the attackers, Lieutenant John H. "Blackie" Parker, after utmost difficulty, had been able to drag his Gatling gun battery down the almost impassable road and place it to the left side of the attacking line. From here he could deliver an enfilading fire into the enemy's trenches. Although his concept was not consistent with tactics being taught at the time, Parker had always felt that rapid-fire guns such as the Gatling gun could prove very effective if they were made a part of the forces assaulting a redoubt.

Several soldiers of the black Tenth Cavalry, who had become separated from their outfit, served as auxiliaries in Lieutenant Parker's Gatling gun unit and performed so well under fire that Parker later stated that they were "the peers of any soldier in the detachment." Sergeant Graham of the black Tenth Cavalry was recommended for a Medal of Honor for his actions while serving with the Gatling gun battery because he had performed very hazardous duty by bringing up ammunition across a fire-swept zone. The medal was not awarded.

Soon after the commencement of Parker's potent Gatling gun firepower, the attacking line reached the summit of the hill since the defending Spaniards had decided to fall back to a second line of trenches below the crest of the hill nearer to Santiago. The assistance provided by the Gatling guns proved decisive in the attack by causing significant and dramatic diminution in the volume of Spanish fire at a crucial moment. Although firing for only eight and a half minutes during the battle, they each poured out bullets at the rate of nine hundred rounds a minute.

On the southern portion of the hill, the black Twenty-fourth Infantry had started its charge at about the same time. Beginning to the extreme left of the American attacking line of battle and storming the heights under a barrage of Spanish bullets, the Twenty-fourth shouted war whoops above the screams and cries of the battlefield and the roar of human yells, appearing to be "an angry mob" oblivious to the death and destruction around them. In a fury, inspired by the slaughter of men around them, the men charged upward, losing four of their officers, who were knocked down within a minute of each other.[37] Captain Ducat, the first to be hit, was killed instantly; then his replacement, Lieutenant Gurney, a Michigan man, was slain on the same spot. Within a few minutes his substitute, Lieutenant Lyon, was shot, to be followed a short time later by the regimental commander, Captain Liscum.

A news telegram of July 6, 1898, reported that the magnificent courage of the Mississippi, Louisiana, Arkansas and Texas black soldiers, the rank and file of the black Twenty-fourth Infantry Regiment, was admired by every officer who had written about the battle. The telegram stated further that white officers of the Twenty-fourth Infantry had always said the Southern black soldier would fight as well as any white man if led by those in whom he had confidence. This question had often been debated, and San Juan Hill offered the first occasion in which this claim could be tested, "in a manner which makes us all proud believers in the truth which their leaders had spoken." More praise for the heroism of the black Twenty-fourth Infantry was forthcoming from a member of the Second Massachusetts Infantry: "They knew no such word as fear, but swept up the hill like a legion of demons."

Confessing a certain prejudice against serving in black regiments, a white lieutenant of the black Ninth Infantry indicated a change of heart: "Do you know, I shouldn't want anything better than to have a company in a Negro regiment? I am from Virginia, and have always had the usual feeling about commanding colored troops. But after seeing that charge of the Twenty-fourth up the San Juan Hill, I should like the best in the world to have a Negro company. They went up that incline yelling and shouting just as I used to hear when they were hunting rabbits in Virginia. The Spanish bullets only made them wilder to reach the trenches." News reports continued to extol the bravery of the Twenty-fourth Infantry: "The Twenty-fourth took the brunt of the fight, and all through it, even when whole companies were left without an officer, not for a moment were these colored soldiers shaken or wavering in the face of the fierce attack made upon them. Wounded Spanish officers later declared that the heaviest Spanish fire was directed at the black troops, because they did not believe the black soldier would stand up against them, and they believed that this was the faulty place in the American line. Never were men more amazed than were the Spanish officers to see the steadiness and cool courage with which the Twenty-fourth charged front forward onto the Tenth Spanish company under the hottest fire. The value of the Negro as a soldier is no longer a debatable question."

The black Tenth Cavalry, in the fight alongside the Rough Riders, received praise from one of its wounded white officers in a report for the Springfield, Illinois, newspaper. Lieutenant Roberts had been lying on the ground, but when he raised up to give an order a bullet passed through his abdomen, making it necessary that he be carried from the field. Later he said: "The heroic charge of the Tenth Cavalry saved the Rough Riders from destruction; and, had it not been for the Tenth Cavalry, the Rough Riders would never have passed through the seething cauldron of Spanish missiles." He further stated: "Those men performed deeds of heroism on that day which have no parallel in the history of warfare. They were under fire from six in the morning until 1:30 in the afternoon, with strict orders not to return the hail of lead, and not a man in those dusky ranks flinched. The brigade was instructed to move forward soon after one o'clock to assault the series of blockhouses which was regarded as impregnable by the foreign attaches. With what cheering did our boys go up that hill! Their naked bodies seemed to present a perfect target to the fire of the dons, but they never flinched. San Juan fell many minutes before El Caney, which had been attacked first, and I think the Negro soldiers can be thanked for the greater part of that glorious work." Lieutenant John J. Pershing spoke of the sentiments among most white officers in charge of black troops on July 1, "We officers of the Tenth Cavalry could have taken our black heroes in our arms. They had again fought their way into our affections, as they here had fought their way into the hearts of the American people." In the same vein, George Kennan, writing in *Campaigning In Cuba*: "It is the testimony of all who saw them under fire that they fought with the utmost courage, coolness and determination."

The abandoned Spanish fortifications yielded a small harvest of food that was carefully divided among the occupying troops. Roosevelt stated in his autobiography that a certain amount of wine and strong spirits had been found along with the food, but he had been able to destroy the "fiery spirits," however, only after inebriation had overcome several of his soldiers. The few Americans who finally occupied the trenches at the top of the hill were vulnerable to counterattack which was not long in coming. Fortunately, when the counterattack did come, enough soldiers of the black Tenth Cavalry and fragments of other regiments had arrived to add backbone to American resistance. It was at about this stage in the battle that Colonel Roosevelt was heard to say to a colleague: "We are within measurable distance of a terrible military disaster."

A Private Smith of the Seventy-first New York Volunteers, commenting on the battle and especially about the performance of the black troops, stated: "I am a Southerner by birth and I never thought much of the colored man. But, somewhat, now I feel differently about them, for I met them in camp, on the battlefield, and that's where a man gets to know a man. I never saw such fighting as those Tenth Cavalry men did. They didn't seem to know what fear was, and their battle hymn was, 'There'll be a hot time in the old town tonight.' That's not a thrilling hymn to hear on the concert stage, but when you are lying in a trench with the smell of powder in your nose and the crack of rifles almost deafening you and bullets tearing up the ground around you like huge hailstones beating down the dirt, and you see before you a blockhouse from which there belches forth the machine gun, pouring a torrent of leaden missiles, while from holes in the ground you see the leveled rifles of thousands of enemies that crack out death in ever-increasing succession and then you see a body of men go up that hill as if it were in drill, so solid do they keep their formation, and those men are yelling, 'There'll be a hot time in the old town tonight,' singing as if they liked their work, why, there's an appropriateness in the tune that kind of makes your blood creep and your nerves to thrill and you want to get up and go ahead, if you lose a limb in the attempt. And that's what those 'niggers' did. You just heard a lieutenant say, 'Men, will you follow me?,' and you hear a tremendous shout answer them, 'You bet we will,' and right up through that death-dealing storm you see men charge, that is, you see them until the darned Springfield rifle powder blinds you and hides them."

One of the the black cavalry soldiers on the heights of San Juan Hill vividly described the assault: "With a yell, which would have done credit to a Comanche Indian, they seemed oblivious to the perfect hailstorm of bullets, the blazing July sun and the barbed wire entanglements as they charged the blockhouse. I was in the fight of July l, and it was in that fight that I received my wound. We were under fire and were without food and with but little water. We had been cut off from our packtrain as the Spanish sharpshooters shot our mules as soon as they came anywhere near the lines, and it was impossible to move supplies. Very soon after the firing began our colonel was killed, and most of our other officers were killed or wounded; so that the greater part of that desperate battle was fought by some of the Ninth and Tenth cavalries without officers or at least, if there were any officers around, we neither saw them nor heard their commands. The last command I heard our captain give was: 'Boys, when you hear my whistle, lie flat down on the ground.' Whether he ever whistled or not I do not know. The next move we made was when, with a terrific yell, we charged up to the Spanish trenches and bayoneted and clubbed them out of their places in a jiffy. Some of the men of our regiment say that the last command they heard was: 'To the rear', but this command they utterly disregarded and charged to the front until the day was won and the Spaniards, those not dead in the trenches, fled back to the city."

Another soldier, William H. Brown of the black Tenth Cavalry, said: "A foreign officer, who was standing near our position when we started out to make that charge, was heard to say: 'Men, for heaven's sake, don't go up that hill! It would be impossible for human beings to take that position! You can't stand the fire!' Notwithstanding this, with a terrific yell we rushed up the enemy's works, and you know the result. Men who saw him said that, when this officer saw us make the charge, he turned his back upon us and wept."

Sergeant George Berry, a thirty-year veteran color-bearer of the black Tenth Cavalry, was able not only to plant the colors of his own regiment on San Juan Hill but simultaneously to set the Third Cavalry Regiment's standard beside it. Berry was the first soldier to reach the blockhouse on San Juan Hill where he hoisted the two flags in a torrent of Spanish bullets. A giant in stature and strength, Berry advanced up the hill and came across the banner of the Third Cavalry lying in the dust, left there after its bearer had been shot. He picked up the fallen banner and, now with two heavy staves to bear, rushed toward the summit yelling like a demon. When he reached the top with the two banners, he was accosted by one of the officers of the Third Cavalry who asked him to return the trophy fairly won by him and his to keep according to the usages of war. With a smile and a few words,

Berry graciously relinquished the banner.

Newspapers, for a few days only, were enthusiastic in their praise of the heroism of black soldiers: "The test of the Negro soldier has been applied, and today the whole world stands amazed at the valor and distinctive bravery shown by the men, who in the face of the most galling fire, rushed onward, while shot and shell tore fearful gaps in their ranks. These men, the Tenth Cavalry, did not stop to ask was it worthwhile to lay down their lives for the honor of the country that has silently allowed her citizens to be killed and maltreated in almost every conceivable way; they did not stop to ask would their dead bring deliverance to their race from mob violence and lynchings. They saw their duty and did it."

As is evident from the writings of both those participating in the battle and of those reporting on the battle, the performance of black troops was outstanding. Many others had similar comments. At a meeting of the Medal of Honor Legion in October 1898, Commanding General of the Army Miles paid tribute to the splendid heroism and soldierly qualities of the men of the Ninth and Tenth Cavalries and the Twenty-fourth and Twenty-fifth Infantry Regiments in the Santiago campaign. He stated that their actions were "without parallel in the history of the world."

Thus the assertion that black soldiers should receive a prominent share of the credit for overcoming the Spaniards in the Battle of San Juan Hill is difficult to refute. Without their numbers, bravery, determination, marksmanship, and experience under fire, it is very unlikely that the assault would have been successful, a conclusion supported by the evidence presented. The heroic performance of Sergeant Major Edward L. Baker, previously mentioned in the introduction to this volume, is but one example of the bravery so common among black soldiers during the battle.[38]

While rallying his men in preparation for the ascent up San Juan Hill, Colonel T. A. Baldwin, riding along the river bank, was suddenly shaken by a large shell exploding nearby. The officer's horse reared, throwing him onto the sandy beach beside the river. Through the smoke, Sergeant Baker saw his colonel leaning against a sand dune holding his arm; so, dodging the rain of bullets and exploding shells which peppered his legs with shrapnel, Baker ran to the wounded officer and knelt beside him to find that shrapnel had entered his commander's arm and side.

Colonel Baldwin insisted the sergeant return to the lines and ordered him to go back and rally the men. Disregarding enemy fire, Baker carried the wounded man to safety and rejoined his men to spend the rest of the day struggling beside them in battle. By now the Americans were defiantly pounding the enemy with heavy rifle fire from behind a clump of bushes near the river bank. On re-entering the fight, over the deafening sound of exploding shells and artillery, Baker heard a desperate cry for help. He looked back through the thick smoke and discovered a fellow soldier in the river, struggling frantically to keep his head above water. Baker dropped his weapon and waded out into the water to grab the helpless soldier and pull him ashore. While running toward the river, a shell passed so close to Baker's head that he could feel its heat. Disregarding the enemy fire, Baker carried the wounded man to safety and again returned to the battle.

In August 1898, Sergeant Baker was commissioned a second lieutenant in the Tenth United States Volunteer Infantry. The promotion was to the rank of brevet lieutenant, meaning that his rank was temporary; however, on July 3, 1902, he was awarded the Medal of Honor for his heroic exploits at San Juan Hill. Only five Medals of Honor were issued to black troops during the entire Cuban War. Sergeant Baker was the only black soldier, in the cavalry or the infantry, to receive a Medal of Honor for bravery exhibited on the open field of battle. As indicated previously, four black cavalrymen of the Tenth Cavalry Regiment received Medals of Honor for heroism shown when they went ashore under very adverse conditions on a small peninsula in another part of Cuba. Although extremely heroic, the action did not take place in the open battlefield, as had been the case with Sergeant Baker.[39]

Serving valorously from the time of its formation in 1869, throughout its fighting in the Indian Wars (against both the Comanches and the Apaches), the war with Spain, and the battles of the Philippine Rebellion, the unhonored black Twenty-fifth Infantry Regiment never had a soldier of such recognized bravery that he received the Medal of Honor. In the Spanish-American War, on the southern slope of San Juan Hill, fighting alongside the black Twenty-fourth Infantry, had been the white Seventeenth Infantry whose soldiers received the astounding number of nine Medals of Honor; whereas the troops of the Twenty-fourth Infantry received none. The black Twenty-fourth Infantry Regiment had previously earned only two medals for bravery during twenty-nine years of Indian Wars, and these two had been awarded not for battlefield bravery but because two enlisted men had been instrumental in breaking up a robbery in the celebrated Wham Payroll Robbery of May 11, 1889.

In an earlier war, George Washington had stated in a certificate awarding the "Badge Of Merit" to a Sergeant Bissell for exceptional bravery as a spy: "It hath ever been an established maxim in the American Service that the Road to Glory was open to All, that Honorary Rewards and Distinctions were the greatest Stimuli to virtuous actions and that distinguished Merit should not pass unnoticed or unrewarded." Unfairness is clearly evidenced by the striking contrast between the number of medals for bravery awarded black troops in the Spanish-American War in comparison to the number awarded white soldiers, a fact reflecting racist attitudes of that day. Of the eighteen Medals of Honor awarded to soldiers for bravery in the Spanish-American War, none was awarded to a black infantryman, even though these black soldiers had been in the forefront of the fighting, both at El Caney and at San Juan Hill.

14

To offer war when they should kneel for peace.

—Shakespeare, *The Taming of the Shrew*

Peace Negotiations

By sunset, July 3, American troops had even more securely fortified their positions atop San Juan Heights, while the leaders of the two armies negotiated. Two days of negotiation finally culminated in a truce that remained in effect for about a week. During the first week in July the rainy season started in earnest, and torrential downpours turned trails and roads into canals of mud. Wagons sank up to their hubs, while men walked in mud up to their knees. So much water remained on the surface of the ground that soldiers slept in the muck with their heads propped up above the water level, and during the day troops walked around naked in the rain after storing what few clothes they had in their rubber ponchos. When General Miles visited one of the troop camps he was much amused by the sight of several hundred entirely nude troops standing at attention and saluting.

General William Shafter, commander of the American forces, must have played a good bit of poker during his Army career, because events proved him to be a master at bluffing. After the truce had been agreed to by the Spaniards, he immediately sent a letter to General Toral, the commanding general of the Spanish forces, demanding an unconditional surrender. When the Spaniards refused the terms of the surrender proposed by General Shafter, the truce ended and preliminary preparations for the assault on Santiago began, although the American forces were by now in no condition for vigorous offensive action. Lieutenant John J. Pershing of the Tenth Cavalry recalled the brief resumption of active fighting: "The battle raged on with the same old fury as of the week preceding, with shells and bullets whistling violently for a few moments." But enemy fire gradually decreased and finally subsided entirely on July 11.

After agreeing to a truce with his poorly equipped troops widely dispersed along the hilltop overlooking Santiago, General Shafter recognized that his forces were so few in number and the trenches so lightly manned that any heavy enemy counterattack would likely overwhelm them. The defenses at the crest of the hill were so vulnerable that he advised the high command in Washington to order withdrawal of his troops toward the coast to allow him to consolidate his forces. The old poker player lacked the confidence that holding a strong hand would have given. Fortunately, his superiors in Washington instructed him to hold his ground, wisely concluding that any retreat would be an indication of military weakness and lack of resolve.

Several days after the Battle of San Juan Hill, having failed to receive a satisfactory response to his first surrender demands, General Shafter decided to draw enemy fire and locate enemy positions by initiating a skirmish close to Santiago, in spite of the paucity of American troops in the battle line. Shafter again showed his particular confidence in the black Twenty-fifth Infantry with whom he had served on the Texas border. After having chosen them to lead the invasion ashore three weeks previously, he now selected two companies of them to start the skirmish.

Deployed in a skirmish line, the troops started their advance while General Shafter watched the movement from a distant hill. He realized, however, that such a skirmish would sacrifice these men without much benefit and had them recalled. It is probable that not a man would have escaped death or serious wounds had the movement been completed. But because of this deployment, the Twenty-fifth Infantry entrenched along a railroad some thousand yards nearer the city than any other regiment and was consequently well-positioned to move into the city when peace was established.

Another letter was sent by General Shafter to General Toral again demanding an unconditional surrender, but terms were once more refused. Shafter's bluff continued. On receiving a negative reply to his latest communication, Shafter threatened the Spanish with reduction of the city of Santiago to rubble by an artillery barrage, although he had so little artillery that this was an empty threat. By this date, the Spanish general had indicated that a surrender might be forthcoming if the Americans assured Spanish troops of free transportation back to Spain, without undue consequences related to their prior military operations.[40]

The Spanish change of heart was brought on by actions of the Spanish fleet blockaded by the American navy in the excellent harbor at Santiago. Admiral Cervera of the Spanish navy had not expected to be caught in the harbor at Santiago when he had anchored his fleet to have a few repairs done and to refuel several months previously. He had planned to leave immediately after fueling and repairs, but the immediate appearance of American warships and interference from military leaders in Havana delayed his departure. Despite his protests, he had been told to remain in the harbor and assist in defense of the shore batteries. A serious shortage of coal for his warships further limited the options available to him. When leaving Spain for the western Atlantic, Admiral Cervera had sent a despairing telegram back to his minister of marine, stating in part: "I beg your Excellency to permit me to insist that the result of our voyage to America must be disastrous for the future of our country." This Spanish admiral knew what the future held in store and realized that his obsolete fleet could be completely destroyed by the American navy.

On Sunday, July 3, at a cost of one American life, the United States fleet destroyed the entire Spanish squadron outside Santiago harbor. To save himself during the debacle, Admiral Cervera jumped overboard to swim from his flagship and was captured along with seventeen hundred Spanish sailors. The only Spanish warship capable of attaining enough speed to escape ran out of coal and was easily destroyed. Following the naval battle, William Randolph Hearst explored the scene while aboard his ship, the *Sylvia*, and discovered a group of twenty-nine Spanish sailors huddled on the shore trying to avoid capture by the murderous Cuban rebels (who had beheaded the Spaniards captured at El Caney). Taking them aboard ship, he fed them and later turned them over to the American navy, from whom he demanded and received a receipt. The date being July 4, he had the pleasure of hearing his captives give three cheers for George Washington.

Similar to the aftermath of the battle for El Caney was the controversy about credit for the victory over the Spanish fleet. Admiral Sampson claimed responsibility for the victory; however it was actually Commodore Schley who had done the real fighting and had smelled the gunsmoke. Unfortunately for Admiral Sampson, he had been ashore attending a strategy conference at the time of the naval battle. Just as in the Battle of El Caney, the higher an officer's rank, the more likely it seems he was to claim credit for victories not won by his own actions in this war, and the less tolerant was he of any dispute to his claim.[41] American victory actually resulted from no particular strategy but was primarily the result of the efforts of naval officers of lower rank, made easy by the very inferior equipment of the Spanish Navy. The Spanish lost their fleet because the wooden decks of their ships caught fire, and the marksmanship of their sailors was extremely poor. Nor was it a triumph of American naval marksmanship, since, of the 9,433 shells fired at the enemy, only 122 hit the target (at that time the maximum range of a battleship's guns was only two thousand yards).

Once the Spanish fleet had been destroyed, General Toral undoubtedly saw the futility of continuing hostilities that would serve no useful purpose and would lead to more loss of life. Under instructions from his government, he signified his intention to cease military action and work toward a permanent peace treaty if certain Spanish conditions were met. Thus the firmness demonstrated by Shafter at the very beginning of negotiations had paid off, and arrangements were made for a meeting between the two commanding generals and their staffs.

When reveille sounded on that Sunday morning, July 10, 1898, half of the great semi-lunar American military camp was awake and eager for a triumphal entry into the city. Speculation was high as to which detachment would accompany the general and his staff into Santiago, with the choice falling upon the Ninth Infantry. With much effort, soldiers hoisted General Shafter onto the back of a horse, and the party, including Generals Lawton, and Wheeler, then moved slowly down the hill to the road leading to Santiago. Outside the city walls the party reached the now-famous tree under which all prior negotiations for the surrender of the city had taken place. When they reached that site, cannon on every hillside and those in the city itself boomed forth a salute of twenty-one guns. Cheer upon cheer arose, running from end to end of the eight miles of American lines. A company of black cavalry and the black Twenty-fifth Infantry then moved forward to join General Shafter and his party. During the ceremony, when protocol dictated that both parties in the ceremony be standing, Shafter indicated that he would participate in the surrender ceremony while still seated on his horse. He evidently had serious doubts about the spectacle he might create by a second attempt at mounting his horse.

In view of the overextended situation of American troops, and because serious disease was already beginning to take its toll, the Americans were amazed and thankful that their opponents had capitulated so readily. Formal surrender documents were signed on July 17, 1898, with weakened Spain losing her tenuous hold on her international role in the European balance of powers. In striking contrast to the pinnacle of wealth and power it had attained two centuries previously, Spain was now relegated to a bit part as the stage of the twentieth century opened.

On August 12, 1898, Secretary Alger cabled orders to all military commanders that a protocol of peace had been signed and that all hostilities should cease. The protocol was signed at 4:23 p.m. at the White House by Secretary of State Day, for the United States, and by M. Cambon, Ambassador of France, representing the Spanish government. Among other things, the protocol specified that five commissioners from each country would meet in Paris no later than October to start drawing up a treaty of peace.

It can truly be said that, for the Americans, gaining victory was "a very close thing," so close, in fact, that President McKinley felt that the war had been terminated under divine guidance, and that the United States had acquired a colonial empire "only under explicit instructions vouchsafed in response to prayer."

15

Whose limbs unburied on the naked shore
Devouring dogs and hungry vultures tore.
—from Alexander Pope's translation of *The Iliad*

Pestilence Takes Its Toll

By the time of the surrender, the physical condition of the American troops had badly deteriorated, and bodies of unburied soldiers were lying in the mud and undergrowth being badly eaten by vultures, who always start their assault on a corpse by pecking out its eyeballs. In competition with the vultures were hordes of Cuban land crabs that completely surround a victim and, when certain that "death's pale flag" is flying, greedily devour what flesh can be found.

A black trooper noted that nearly all the officers had either been wounded or "had played out" and gone, leaving the exhausted enlisted men hungry and almost naked. All were suffering acutely from inadequate supplies of medicine, food, and potable drinking water. The uninterrupted and rapid spread through the entire army of yellow fever, malaria and dysentery caused a daily increase in the number of deaths and of those desperately ill.[42] One black cavalryman observed that many of his comrades had become so emaciated as to be barely recognizable. While the climate and diseases of Cuba took a frightful toll among black soldiers, the mortality was even greater among the white men, which, to one observant black trooper, showed beyond a doubt that colored troops could stand any hardships the whites could.

Due to a serious deficiency of supplies and personnel, conditions in the American hospitals were nothing short of horrible, because medical facilities were overburdened by the many wounded as well as by those suffering from the ravages of severe and frequently fatal intestinal diseases. Added to these problems was the need to care for those suffering from the tropical diseases of malaria and yellow fever that had begun to make their presence felt within two weeks of the invasion. On July 26, 1898, slightly over a month after the invasion, yellow fever was reported to have stricken 639 more troops than on the day before, while on the next day another 822 were listed as having the disease, bringing the total to 3,193 cases (20 percent of the invasion forces).

Among the most remarkable persons involved in this brief war was a seventy-two year old lady with unlimited enthusiasm and energy. Clara Barton had become famous during the Civil War for her efforts at easing the suffering of wounded soldiers, and, when the International Red Cross had been officially incorporated in Switzerland shortly after the Franco-Prussian War, Clara Barton was one of its most enthusiastic leaders.

During the years leading to the Spanish-American War it was evident to the entire world that many Cubans were dying from starvation and disease due to being imprisoned in Spanish concentration camps. At the vigorous urging of Clara Barton, President McKinley, with the concurrence of the Spanish ambassador, finally officially authorized the Red Cross in January 1898 to take food and supplies to Cuba to minister to the needs of the starving "reconcentrados." So at the age of 72, Miss Barton landed in Havana, where, on January 13, 1898, she was a luncheon guest aboard an American warship, the *Maine*. On February 15, the *Maine* exploded and sank, thwarting her plans to aid the Cuban peasants; however she did visit the camps of the imprisoned peasants where she was appalled at the numbers of those dead and dying from starvation.

After war was declared in April, Miss Barton was officially appointed director of distribution of all aid to the Cuban peasants, so she spent April to June 1898 in Key West, Florida (where she was visited by the journalist George Kennan and his wife). Impatient to get into action, she returned to Washington and leased a former supply ship, *The State of Texas*, to be used by the Red Cross in its mission of mercy in Cuba. From Santiago she made a brief side trip to Guantanamo to tend to the needs of the wounded following the first battle with the Spanish, and it was here that she had the pleasure of seeing, for the first time, Red Cross personnel treating wounded while wearing their Red Cross brassards.

When the American navy had thoroughly defeated the Spanish, Clara Barton was astonished and much pleased when Admiral Sampson notified her that her ship could be the first ship to enter the harbor at Santiago. It entered the harbor late one afternoon and remained the only ship anchored there that evening, to be joined the next day by the American fleet that anchored nearby. Her enthusiasm at being so honored was tempered to a degree when Commodore Schley (no friend of the admiral) told her, possibly in jest, that the admiral might have been using her ship as a mine sweeper to be certain that no mines had been left in the harbor by the Spaniards.

After returning to the invasion port of Siboney, Red Cross personnel were at first denied access to the abandoned hospital buildings being prepared for American soldiers. Undaunted, she put her people to work preparing a hospital for the Cuban wounded and did such an impressive job that, three days later, the Americans relented and requested the Red Cross to assist them in cleaning their hospital. From that time on the Red Cross worked for both Cubans and Americans.

During this period, the still vigorous Clara Barton was seen many times perched high up on wagons loaded with bales and bundles just as she had done during the Civil War. General Shafter gave her a document authorizing her to commandeer any wagon or mules she thought necessary to carry out her mission to transport supplies and medicines to field hospitals. Frustrated by the shortage of medical supplies and personnel, Miss Barton felt she had been seriously misled by the War Department that had told her it was fully prepared to handle all casualties. Had she known this was the figment of some bureaucrat's imagination, she could have brought more supplies and more manpower on her leased vessel. With the end of active fighting, she became administrator of the fever hospital at Siboney to help care for the ever-expanding number of fever victims.[43]

Because of his interest in yellow fever, Major William Gorgas had been appointed as medical officer in charge of the yellow fever hospital at Siboney. At that time he had rejected the theory of some of his colleagues that mosquitoes transmitted the disease; so he did what many American cities had been doing for years to prevent the contagion: he lit a huge bonfire in the hope that germs of yellow fever would be destroyed by smoke and flames. Later, Gorgas was to become the sanitary officer for Havana.[44]

At Siboney, where there had been an initial attempt to segregate the merely wounded from those suffering from pestilence, the large mass of sick people made triage impossible. The hospital camp was so crowded, so full of rubbish, and in such horrible condition from previous Cuban occupancy that it was an Augean task to achieve even a semblance of cleanliness. Surgeons, nurses, and hospital stewards were themselves quite ill while circulating among the mass of suffering and dying humanity lying in the filth of the fetid pest-house.

Demonstrating altruism worthy of the highest accolades, soldiers of the black Twenty-fourth Infantry took on the task of assisting in care of patients in the pestilential yellow fever hospital at Siboney. So grave were the risks associated with such a job that, before the Twenty-fourth Infantry volunteered to take the duty, eight other regiments had been offered the hospital assignment but had refused.

Doctor LaGarde, chief medical officer in the hospital, assembled the entire regiment and carefully explained the desperate need for help in caring for the sick and wounded, at the same time clearly pointing out the risks related to nursing patients with yellow fever and other potentially fatal diseases. Major Markley, the commanding officer, then asked for volunteers, and, much to his surprise and pleasure, the whole regiment stepped forward. Seventy-five volunteers composed the first team of volunteer medical corpsmen, but within a few days many had fallen sick to be replaced by another group of the same size.

With the passage of days, almost everyone in the regiment became ill. In spite of this, each time a shortage of manpower developed due to illness and more volunteers were asked for, the whole of the remaining group stepped forward. The morning report of one day listed 241 of the 456 men in the regiment as being on sick call. Captain Charles Dodge died from exposure to disease while working in the hospital, as did thirty-five of the enlisted men while performing voluntary duty in the service of their fellow-man.

A newspaper correspondent wrote that the battle the regiment fought in the pestilential hospital "was even more gallant than its action on the battlefield." It was certainly more costly in lives affected, because of the 456 troops volunteering for work in the yellow fever hospital only twenty-four escaped sickness. The black Twenty-fourth Infantry remained on duty at the pestilential hospital for some forty-one days until it was relieved and marched to the train with only nine officers and 198 men of its original fifteen officers and 456 enlisted men.

Bravery can be exhibited in many ways. The intrepid soldier charging headlong against a well-fortified enemy exhibits bravery strengthened and enhanced by the orders given by his officers, by endocrine and other physical changes taking place in his body, and by the team spirit and enthusiasm of those joining him in the attack. Even greater heroism is exhibited by those who, after careful reflection, elect to expose themselves to possible death, each minute and hour of the day, by a deliberate election to care for sick persons whose illness is not only frequently fatal, but contagious and caused by an unknown agent.

Ministering such service in the face of constant peril was the selfless and noble-minded choice of black soldiers of the Twenty-fourth Infantry, a demonstration of personal sacrifice meriting the highest praise, of which there was little.

Vigorously objecting to an order received from Secretary Alger on August 4, 1898, to move his army to San Luis in the interior of the island, General Shafter wrote in a telegram to his superiors that if this transfer occurred "the men would die like rotten sheep." He stated that the army must be moved at once or perish. In a more threatening vein only six weeks after the first troops had landed in Cuba, he noted that the persons preventing such a move would be held responsible for the unnecessary loss of many thousands of lives because "90 percent of the army is now stricken with yellow fever or malaria, and the situation is growing more frightful." Shafter said he was writing because he could not bear to see his men, who had fought so nobly and had endured such extreme hardships and danger so uncomplainingly, go to destruction without his striving "as far as lies in my power to avert a doom as fearful as it is unnecessary and undeserved."

The Tampa newspaper of August 7 reported that in Cuba on August 3, the total number of sick was 3,778, of which 2,589 were suffering from "fever," and there had been reported 449 new cases. Nine deaths had occurred, making this the largest daily mortality to that time. On the following day 3,354 were reported sick, of whom 2,589 had "fever," and the number of deaths had risen to fifteen. The rising death rate was a cause for considerable alarm, and every effort was being made to hasten the troops' departure from the diseased tropics.

One month after hostilities had ceased, on August 7, General Shafter again requested that the Fifth Army Corps be transferred from Cuba. At the time, casualty figures showed that the army had lost 243 men in combat and 771 to disease, with even more deaths to occur after the corps had been transferred to the salubrious climate of Long Island. Machinations that did result in withdrawal of American troops from Cuba could lead one to the definite conclusion that Colonel Roosevelt had influence in military operations disproportionate to his rank.

If things were not going according to Roosevelt's wishes, he seemed able to change them by merely ignoring the command structure of the War Department, or by appealing to the American public through his well-honed newspaper contacts. No better example of this is the insubordinate way in which he and the other senior officers in Cuba tried to hasten the decision by the War Department and the secretary of the army to order withdrawal of the main mass of troops from Cuba and to station them at Montauk, Long Island. General Shafter called a meeting of his medical officers and senior line officers to discuss the health situation of the troops, and the consensus was that there was an urgent need for evacuation of the army in spite of the War Department's seeming unwillingness to take action. In Washington the government's reason for deferring a decision regarding evacuation of the troops was that terms of the peace treaty with Spain had not yet been agreed to by both parties. American political leaders were therefore anxious not to appear precipitous in removing American troops from Cuba, because to do so might weaken their bargaining position.

Roosevelt volunteered to write a letter, signed by all senior officers, stating that they were unanimous in their opinion that the Army should be immediately transferred to the northern United States because of the heavy toll being taken by malaria and yellow fever. It stated that the Army must be moved at once, or perish. The letter, later called the "round-robin letter," was immediately released by Roosevelt to the Associated Press and was published the following morning in American newspapers, an action that enraged President McKinley as well as the Secretary of War Alger.[45] Publication of the information that the American army was in dire straits could have had serious consequences, if the Spanish had used the knowledge to either demand changes in the terms of the cease-fire agreement or refused to sign the treaty, thus prolonging the war. There was even talk of a court-martial for Colonel Roosevelt, but within three days orders were forthcoming for his desired evacuation of the troops.

16

Many brave men lived before . . . but all are overwhelmed in eternal night, unwept, unknown, because they lacked a sacred poet.

—Horace, *Odes*

A Turning Point In History

There are similarities between the failure of black soldiers in the Union Army after the Civil War to receive favorable recognition for their efforts and the dearth of acclaim given to blacks after the Spanish-American War. Although nearly two hundred thousand black troops with white officers fought for the Union during the Civil War and demonstrated great heroism in several battles, it is only recently that historians have brought to light their very significant participation in the war. Strongly prejudiced individuals after the Civil War actively hushed-up reports favorable to blacks. After the Spanish-American War, a brief flurry of praise for black heroism was swept away by the whirlwind of violent racial turmoil that occupied the minds and emotions of white Americans for many years thereafter.

The essential premise of this book is that the Spanish-American War ended in victory for the Americans as a result of the efforts of black soldiers. Their contribution to the history of that war has not been adequately noted because of a combination of faulty and biased newspaper reporting[46] combined with widespread racial prejudice among white Americans who did not make the effort to further explore the evidence about black heroism that was briefly publicized in newspapers during the war. Already presented is evidence of the black soldiers' heroism, and now there remains the necessity to explain its consequences and why it is not general knowledge.

Following the Spanish-American War, there were reports of economic possibilities for black Americans in the Caribbean Islands, but this did not prove of interest to blacks who had seen first-hand the poverty and poor living conditions of the Cubans. The American victory over the Spanish was also a victory for the predominantly black population of Cuba. Thus there had developed another opportunity for descendants of slaves in their ineluctable rise from degradation to positions of wealth and influence. Most black Americans, however, were more concerned with the effect the performance of black soldiers would have on them as citizens residing in the States. Black soldiers hoped that their role in rescuing Cuba from Spanish rule would create a more favorable racial climate in America, one that would bring about a stronger belief in the potential of the black race.[47]

Some black editors were so misty-eyed as to believe that brave deeds performed by black soldiers on the battlefield not only would open the way for black soldiers to receive commissions in the regular army, but would also make it possible for all black Americans to enjoy the inalienable rights of citizenship. Voicing this hope was a black editor in Wichita who wrote about the most extravagant hopes of black Americans when he declared that the war with Spain meant more to the black man "than anything since the morning stars sang together. It will shape his destiny as a citizen and bring him up to the full measure of a man the world over."

Because the evidence is persuasive that America could not have achieved victory without the participation of black soldiers, it is especially tragic that black competence and heroism were quickly forgotten in the States, because of ardent racism reinforced by media hyperbole that only strengthened the polarization of the races. America's gradual increase in influence on the international scene can be attributed directly to its involvement in the war with Spain, yet the most persecuted segment of the American population has still not received the recognition it has earned for making this possible. Unfortunately for the aspirations of black Americans, later racial disturbances resulted in such a backlash of animosity toward blacks that any hope of significant change was extinguished.

To understand the flimsiness of the public's knowledge about this war, one must comprehend the complex conditions of the United States in 1898. Prejudice against blacks was reaching ever greater heights throughout the nation, especially in the South. This made it difficult for even an unbiased newsman to find a receptive audience for any copy that extolled or even recognized the heroism and achievements of the black soldier.

Possibly as important as the rise in racial intolerance was the acrimonious newspaper war being waged between William Randolph Hearst and Joseph Pulitzer. Their two newspaper chains were absorbed in a circulation war, aggressively expanding their readership and competing at every turn in all large cities for news or imagined news. From this all-out competition between two corporate giants came frequent incorrect reportage and sometimes intentional deception.

The Spanish-American War, called "The Newspaper War," has been blamed on the cupidity of the mighty newspaper moguls. It has been suggested that Hearst actually instigated the blowing up of the battleship *Maine*, which if not true is at least plausible, and illustrates the extremes to which the reading public believed he might go to create a news event.

The war between the expanding rival newspaper chains took many turns. In early June 1898, Hearst filed a suit against Pulitzer's *New York Herald*, claiming that he had been libeled by a report in the *Herald* stating that one of his boats had been taken into federal custody when Hearst's journal dispatch boat had been stopped in Tampa Bay and boarded by a corporal and military guard. The correspondent on board was said to be suspected of possessing stolen government documents and had plans to head out to sea to send the stolen material by wire. Hearst was incensed at the allegations and saw his chance to weaken his opposition. At a time when a daily newspaper sold for only three cents (five cents for a Sunday edition), the amount of damages claimed was the very large sum of five hundred thousand dollars.[48]

In any case, the reporting of events related to the war's beginning was so distorted and inflammatory that Americans were whipped into a frenzy by what they read in their newspapers.

Arousal of the deep-seated emotions of the ordinary American resulted in a groundswell of enthusiasm for war that politicians could not resist.

A golden age for newspapers had arrived. As the only medium available for quick circulation of news and armed with the news-gathering capacity of the newly perfected telegraph, newspaper chains were poised for explosive expansion. The ocean cable was a new arrival on the scene, enabling one to instantly report events from distant corners of the world and providing the thrilling experience of reading today what had happened yesterday half a world away. When war did occur, newspaper reporters descended like locusts on the army in Tampa, where many of them set up telegraphic bases, while others had communication centers at various cities in Florida or on islands in the Caribbean. In spite of the strictures of a censorship bureau established by the military, such bases were designed to quickly transmit to the northern press any and all news about the war. Larger and better-financed newspapers reinforced their established telegraph bases with a team of reporters who were to stay with the armed forces and feed any information considered to be newsworthy by telegraph to the main office. But the quick ending of the war was disastrous financially for the newspaper chains, which had spent much money in establishing communication networks and hiring armies of reporters. Circulation began to drop as soon as the war was over.

Because communications in Cuba were so extremely difficult due to jungles and unfamiliar terrain, it was the lucky reporter who found himself at a location that gave him any overall perspective of military strategy and operations. During the battles themselves, the location of a reporter determined what he could report with any degree of truth, and the truth was frequently distorted because of strong ambitions and the need to produce copy. In addition, all reporting was against a background of underlying, if not overt, prejudice against blacks.

The most influential newspapers had purchased or leased small yachts or commercial vessels to take the writings of their staff to a telegraph office in the Caribbean or Florida for immediate transmittal to the newspaper. Reporters had available no cable or telephone connections from Cuba to send their dispatches, and the very cumbersome system put pressure on the individual reporter to report something, even if it was wrong. Such a primitive system inevitably resulted in a high volume of very inaccurate news from the battle zone. The reporters' chief sources of news were either soldiers involved in battles or other reporters, but these sources were biased or very narrow in the scope of their information.

The army had not yet started the practice of holding press briefing sessions, as has been the case in subsequent wars; so the absence of background information caused reporters, despite their numbers (estimated at five hundred in Cuba during the war), to describe the war in isolated segments. The very short duration of the military action on land undoubtedly contributed to the confusion of any reporter finding himself in a strange tropical land. Slanted reporting was epidemic. The lion's share of stories was about that central actor on the stage of warfare, Theodore Roosevelt, who well knew the value of an enthusiastic and creative press. Roosevelt was especially fortunate; because General Shafter, who under ordinary circumstances would have at least shared the spotlight with Roosevelt, had made it clear to the correspondents prior to landing his troops ashore that he did not like newspaper personnel. Evidence of his ill will was his confrontation with Hearst correspondent Richard Harding Davis, who had wanted to go ashore from the invasion fleet soon after it had arrived. Davis protested to Shafter about his order temporarily prohibiting any of the eighty-seven newsmen who had accompanied him from going ashore. (The majority of reporters found ways to get ashore despite Shafter's interdiction by persuading those manning the small landing craft to slip them into their load of troops or supplies.) Davis, on telling Shafter that he was a descriptive writer rather than a reporter, was curtly rebuffed: "I don't give a damn who you are."[49]

The press was eager to find a person who could be a celebrity for their newspaper readers at home, and Roosevelt and his troops fit the role perfectly. Since his troops were such a motley group of persons from every stratum of society, whose only common bond was horsemanship, their newsworthiness was outstanding. Richard Harding Davis added considerably to the volume of news concerning Roosevelt, since he was not only a skilled writer but Roosevelt's personal friend. Davis also never failed to add to his communiques, when possible, negative comments about General Shafter. A former managing editor of *Harper's Weekly*, Davis, publisher of many short stories and several novels, had visited Santiago de Cuba before the war and therefore had the advantage of being familiar with its layout.

Some of the mass of newspaper reporters that invaded Cuba did at times report favorably on the military achievements of black soldiers, but such news reporting was desultory. Local communications were nonexistent in Cuba, with sheer luck determining what each individual reporter saw. This situation made it difficult to accurately determine which of the troops and officers were fighting valiantly and which were sitting on the sidelines. Had Shafter been more cooperative, it seems certain that the press would have been more effective and, with some briefing and support from Shafter, might have found it easier to make plans and to obtain transportation in order to witness events first hand. As evidence of Shafter's extreme suspicion of the press and his underlying hostility to their mission, he had all reporters for the Hearst newspaper chain arrested and sent home because of publication of an inflammatory poster that, in his view, might have precipitated a massacre of Spanish prisoners. The capricious expulsion from Cuba took place on July 17, 1898, and because Shafter refused to let them return, proved to be a permanent banning of Hearst representatives from the island.[50] Thus it became even less likely that such reporters would write a recapitulation of events related to the land battles that might, under different circumstances, have contained some reference to the heroism of the black soldiers.

The Springfield, Illinois, black newspaper, the *Record,* of August 13, 1898, voiced its concern that the contribution of black soldiers in the war had been all but ignored by white editors, and, as a consequence, black soldiers would be denied the place in history to which their magnificent service in the war entitled them. It was argued that future generations of black Americans would, as a result, be entirely ignorant of the crucial role their ancestors had played in the war with Spain. Another Springfield paper of that time, the *Republican,* stated that it was shameful how the distinguished record of black troops had been ignored by white editors.

Furthermore, at the turn of the century newspapers were sensitive to their audience and simply did not feel that there was a market for black heroism; consequently, they concentrated on the activities of white troops, especially the five hundred Rough Riders. Any effort at balanced reporting could not have failed to have revealed the essential contribution made by blacks during the war, without which the war would assuredly have been lost, or at least converted into a slow, arduous campaign marked by a staggering loss of American lives from yellow fever and malaria. Had the conflict dragged on for many months it could have become the nineteenth century equivalent of the Viet Nam War, for in the States there were more than two hundred thousand volunteers mobilized and being trained for military action. If they had been sent to Cuba, an ever escalating mortality, primarily from disease, would certainly have proven intolerable to the American public, who would have then demanded some sort of cessation of hostilities. The consequences of a prolonged campaign in Cuba would undoubtedly have resulted in a mortality rate from disease equal to or greater than that of the Spanish Army in Cuba in 1897.

Without a clear-cut victory by the United States, the final peace terms would have reflected the results of the stalemate and caused loss of American prestige, with accompanying unfavorable economic and political consequences. The final peace treaty would have been much less favorable to American interests than those actually achieved by total victory. The treaty agreements regarding Cuba, Puerto Rico, and the Philippines could have taken a very different turn, an outcome that would have radically altered the course of events of American history in the twentieth century. The Philippines and Puerto Rico would probably still be under the hegemony of Spain—or in the empire of one of the more powerful, predatory imperialistic European nations. More important than this would have been the profound influence on America's international relations. Few Americans were emotionally prepared for the consequences of victory with its expanded obligations and unaccustomed problems that attended the country's new and unavoidable responsibilities in the world.

Although events had conspired over a short time to drive America into war with Spain, isolationism still had a very strong following at the end of the nineteenth century. Anti-imperialists (isolationists) shared strong convictions about the posture the United States should adopt and maintain in international affairs and purists among them simply cited the Constitution of the United States: the government should govern only with the informed consent of those governed.

While those opposing isolationism (the expansionists, the imperialists, or the internationalists) may have had some uncertainty as to the eventual outcome of their efforts to immerse the United States in the quagmire of involvement in the affairs of other nations, it is clear from a study of history that once such a course is pursued there is an inevitable increasing commitment to an expanding role in international matters.

The beginning of America's rise from obscurity to world power created a problem for those who thought that the sincere advice of George Washington and Thomas Jefferson should be respected: that America should make every effort to shun involvement with European nations and never take over a foreign nation without the consent of its citizens. Given America's history of carving a civilization out of a wilderness, of throwing off the yoke of Great Britain, and of problems with Spain and France earlier in the century, there was a natural psychological impulse toward isolationism. Additionally, the geography of America predisposed it toward remaining separate from other nations, especially those in Europe whose ancient animosities and conflicting economic aspirations made them seem unattractive partners for any permanent alliance. Fear of Old World wars exacerbated the country's wariness of foreign entanglements to such an extent that the United States had often forcefully reiterated its conviction that its sole area of interest was its hegemony in the Western Hemisphere. One might say that at the beginning of the twentieth century the United States tip-toed into the world.

When the Spanish-American War started, hundreds of prominent American citizens rose up in wrath at the involvement of the United States in war with a European nation. Among those politicians taking this stand were former Secretary of State John Sherman, Senator Ben Tillman, presidential candidate William Jennings Bryan, and many others. University professors in large numbers, labor leaders including Samuel Gompers, and many rich industrialists were among the anti-imperialists of the day. Of these, Andrew Carnegie was the most influential and probably the most effective, although he later lost the "true faith" when he indicated it was perhaps desirable to control the Caribbean islands but not the Philippines. Among the many influential anti-imperialist writers were Mark Twain, William Dean Howells and Edgar Lee Masters.

Dewey's victory at Manila so stunned the anti-imperialists that one of them commented that, while Dewey had lost only one man as a result of the battle, the anti-imperialists had temporarily lost most of their manpower due to a surge of belligerent fervor. Between 1898 and 1900, however, there was a very thorough and careful examination, by both citizens and government, of the advantages and disadvantages of a policy of expansionism (as imperialism was also called). While no referendum was held to give accurate numbers, the forces embracing each opposing philosophy seem to have been about equal in number; so, to a certain extent, the direction of American foreign policy hung in the balance and was, in fact, determined by the outcome of the war with Spain.

Had that war been lost, or had it been a prolonged stalemate with an intolerable loss of life, the anti-imperialists would have become a potent political force, leaving the most xenophobic strain of isolationism in an excellent position to set the course of American foreign policy for at least the next thirty-five years. One might say that "The Viet-Nam Syndrome" (a present-day manifestation of isolationism) would have strongly influenced the attitudes of Americans some seventy years before it actually did.

A natural question to ask is, if the details presented in this history of the Spanish-American War are correct, why doesn't one find them in the standard texts describing the war? One must realize that 1898 was only slightly more than thirty years after the Civil War, and that only forty years previously most black Americans had been slaves. The true role of black Americans had yet to be settled in the minds of the vast majority of white Americans, who had really not come to grips with the profound adjustments necessary in their attitudes and actions if the black man were really to be accepted in American society. Even now, almost a hundred years later, many questions remain unanswered, although there are many reasons for optimism. It is ironic that, at a time when the white American public's respect for black people was at an all-time low, a small group of dedicated, patriotic, black Americans was setting the stage for America's rise to world supremacy. Given the low esteem in which blacks were held by the vast majority of Americans at the end of the nineteenth century, it is not surprising that stories relating to heroism of black soldiers would not have been considered a very marketable commodity. Doubtless, the widely publicized racial turmoil prior to the war, caused by black soldiers' brief but eventful stays in both Chattanooga and Tampa, had left a bitter residue of distaste in the minds of the vast majority of Americans.

Napoleon once said: "History is a set of lies agreed upon." The most reasonable explanation for the failure of historians to recognize and appreciate the black soldiers' essential role in winning the war is that the fighting on land lasted less than two weeks, a brief period during which black soldiers displayed the exceptional heroism that tipped the balance in favor of the Americans. Moreover, the fighting on the battlefield was preceded by several months of bloody racial turmoil in the States in which blacks had been subjected to the severe and stringent segregation practices of Tampa and Chattanooga. Added to the pre-war racial conflict was even more intense and more prolonged turmoil between the races for many years after the Spanish-American War. Widespread and inflammatory newspaper publicity, describing in lurid detail every aspect of these confrontations, gave no hint that the black soldiers' actions may at times have been justified. Both educated and uneducated white Americans felt threatened and puzzled by that stalwart black soldier who embodied something of an enigma. He was thought to be ignorant, immoral and prone to illegal acts, while his uniform, his obvious self-esteem and sturdy military bearing gave him an aura of authority and superiority that proved insufferable to the prejudiced white person.

It is hard for us today—even those of us who lived through the Civil Rights Movement of the 1950s and 1960s—to comprehend the racial climate of the late 1800s and early 1900s. Reconstruction history was successfully revised during the first fifteen years of this century, leaving us sanitized views of slavery and a distorted picture of post-Civil War policies and customs. Immediately after the war, the provisional governments in most of the Southern states implemented laws aimed at controlling the newly freed black labor force. Provisions of these Black Codes authorized involuntary servitude in cases of "vagrancy," and otherwise severely restricted blacks' mobility and ability to own property.

Congressional Reconstruction negated many of the Black Codes, but after white Southerners regained control of the political process in the 1870s, the involuntary labor provisions were reinstituted in many states. A network of laws and social customs gradually evolved to replace slavery with two rigidly separated societies. Beginning in South Carolina in 1895, a complicated system of poll taxes and voter registration disfranchised blacks throughout the South. In 1896, the "separate but equal" doctrine was upheld by the U.S. Supreme Court in the case of *Plessy v. Ferguson*, leaving blacks—especially below the Mason–Dixon Line—in a situation not far removed from slavery. Vestiges of the Black Codes thus remained a part of Southern life and laws until the 1960s.

Along with legal and social segregation came levels of violence that seem unbelievable just a few decades removed. Brutal racial encounters occurred with numbing regularity. Starting in the late 1880s, the number of recorded lynchings reached staggering and sickening proportions, to a peak of 226 in 1892, only to gradually recede over the next fifty or sixty years. The wave of racism was surging forward in 1900, just when black soldiers who had performed so well in the Spanish-American War were hoping to enjoy recognition from white Americans for their efforts in the war. Their heroics would be ignored, partly because Americans and their leaders were not only unready for elevation of the status of blacks but were wrestling with the many problems related to a deeper involvement in international affairs.

To make matters worse, after a war of two weeks duration, military ranks were swollen by large numbers of enlistees to a total strength of 274,717 men. At the end of September 1898, the high command of the Army decided that both regular and volunteer black troops should be stationed in the eastern United States, a radical change from the policy in existence prior to the war when black troops had always been stationed west of the Mississippi. Except for a brief time in the post Civil War period, army policy had been strongly enforced to keep black soldiers in the West. Members of Congress at times had intervened when the army had threatened to station blacks in the east (the influential Senator Proctor of Vermont had stated that the most arduous task of his entire political career was his fight, during the Cleveland administration, to keep black troops out of Fort Ethan Allen).

The laws and customs of the Southeast and Texas, especially those related to segregation, were a source of perplexity and animosity to blacks. Each town or city in the South that had a troop of black soldiers stationed nearby experienced frequent, violent, racial explosions between townsfolk and black troops, because the mind of the South remained frozen in the amber of bigotry and racial intolerance. The period immediately after the Spanish-American War was one of the high points of racism in American history, reaching a zenith during the administration of Woodrow Wilson. (The 1915 showing of a new motion picture, *The Birth of a Nation*, aside from being a breakthrough in moviemaking technique, presented a hateful racist message based on a Reconstruction-era book and sparked race riots in at least five cities, as well as being used as a recruiting tool by the Ku Klux Klan.)

Strong prejudice against blacks was so rampant that a group of black soldiers escorting a charge of Spanish prisoners from Tampa to Fort McPherson, Georgia, drew crowds wherever they stopped. These crowds showed more interest in taunting the black soldiers than in viewing the Spanish prisoners. Among those taunting the black guards was a Catholic priest, serving as minister to the Spanish prisoners, who declared later: "It is an outrage that white men [Spaniards] have been subjected to the humiliation of having Negro guards over them." There was evidence of even more virulent prejudice on the part of the citizens of Huntsville, Alabama, who had great difficulty in adjusting to the presence of that most valorous of the black troops, the Tenth Cavalry. Almost daily racial confrontations in Huntsville caused occasional bloodshed, as well as the deaths of two cavalrymen. One citizen of Huntsville, a black man, was arrested for attempting to kill a soldier of the Tenth Cavalry. On being questioned as to why he should be killing one of his own race, he replied that money was being offered for each black cavalryman killed—on public display in Huntsville, in December 1898, had been a poster that promised payment of a bounty to anyone who killed a black soldier. The effects of racial intolerance were pervasive and were aggravated by the widespread newspaper publicity given to each of the frequent episodes of racial conflagration.

After returning to Florida from Cuba, black troops were involved in almost daily racial incidents enthusiastically reported by the press. By force or threat, black soldiers were frequently able to bring about the release of comrades thought to have been unfairly jailed. Perhaps the most serious of these incidents occurred the night the Ninth Cavalry was to travel from Tampa to Montauk Point, New York. One of their number had been arrested on what the black cavalrymen considered to have been a trumped-up charge; so some five companies of well-armed cavalrymen, "who apparently had the sanction of the white officers in command of them," stormed the jail and released their comrade. Shortly thereafter the black soldiers had to face down a large crowd of irate white citizens and police who, realizing that they were overpowered, allowed the prisoner to rejoin his comrades. The cavalrymens' train, departing for New York, had been forcefully stopped by what the local newspaper called "negro ruffians and black brutes," and the engineer had been held at rifle point until the rescuers had returned with their liberated comrade.

The episode caused great hostility in Tampa. At a mass meeting several days later, the absent white officers of the black soldiers were verbally castigated for permitting the affair to happen in their presence. Numerous resolutions were passed, one of which, addressed especially to the officers of the United States Army of whom they had all been so proud, concluded that "the conduct of this regiment brings shame to everyone, save to those who are dead to the sense of it." The governor of Florida was criticized for not making more vigorous efforts to have those thought guilty brought back to Florida for trial.

On August 12, 1898, the *Morning Tribune* of Tampa, noting in a brief article that the people of Lakeland had been able to protect their jail from rescue attempts by black soldiers, stated:

"The black brutes wearing the uniforms of the Tenth United States Cavalry, who have been camped at Lakeland for some time, have at last received orders for departure to Montauk Point, Long Island." Demagogues seized on such incidents, which resulted in even more racism and bigotry. Meanwhile, black soldiers were becoming more determined to resist such discrimination, which increased fears of white Southerners and reduced what little resistance to racism might have existed.

Other racial conflicts after the war included several incidents in Cuba. The most serious and most highly publicized of these resulted from the theft of a pig in the city of San Luis, Cuba, where a company of volunteer black troops had been stationed. When the owner of the purloined pig tried to retrieve his property he was assaulted and killed, and the local police station was attacked. Extensive publicity was given to this outbreak of lawlessness, with the media sparing no effort to picture the black soldier as a villain who could not be trusted to control himself except under strong white leadership.

The presence of so large a contingent of black soldiers in Florida after the war and the problems related thereto probably hardened the attitudes of diehard racists among the white population and caused questions to arise in the minds of moderates as to whether blacks could be assimilated in the culture of predominantly white America. As is true today, a majority of whites realized that the country was founded on the premise that all citizens are equal and every effort must be made to see that this ideal becomes a reality. Racial violence, unfortunately, is a complex issue in which both sides frequently share blame.

This history is not a hagiography in which blacks are to be considered entirely without responsibility for certain events, but for years violent racial incidents continued to occur at regular intervals, and blacks were always the ones accused of being the instigators of violence. There were enough instances of unreasonable black violence to cause an unreasoning public to think that all racial incidents were initiated by blacks. Always to the disparagement of black soldiers, the press publicized and highlighted racial episodes, further convincing the nation that such soldiers were inferior and not worthy to remain in the armed forces, much less to be officers in leadership positions.

It seems without question that the long sequence of racial incidents—starting in April 1898, when the first black troops arrived in Chattanooga, and continuing for many years after the war, in the eastern United States and Cuba—caused a wave of revulsion and deep misgivings on the part of white Americans. Racial troubles in cities, when combined with sensational press coverage, create a potent mix that strongly influences attitudes of the public. When the media was less than evenhanded in such coverage (especially true in the early part of this century), blacks had little or no opportunity to explain the reasons for the trouble. They were automatically considered guilty in the eyes of the public, although underlying inequities and injustices were given little or no recognition.

And this is where my story comes full circle. In 1906, a confrontation between white citizens and black soldiers, the so-called "Brownsville Affair," took place in Texas, resulting in the death of one white man and the injury of another. Black soldiers were summarily blamed for the casualties in what would much later prove to have been a frame-up by a handful of local citizens.[51] Although white officers had testified that their troops were on the base at the time of the trouble, the city mayor and other influential citizens stated otherwise. Spent cartridge shells, later shown to have come from a-nearby firing range, were part of the planted evidence. So much national attention was drawn to the affair, however, that President Theodore Roosevelt finally capitulated to the mounting political pressure and ordered 167 black soldiers discharged from the Army without honor. According to a statement from the Roosevelt White House, these men were guilty of a "conspiracy of silence."

The president's political expedience was upheld by a Senate committee; however, four senators voted against approval of the president's action. I was surprised during my research to learn that one of the dissenters was Senator Morgan Bulkeley of Connecticut, who happens to have been my mother's great-uncle. Senator Bulkeley, in opposition to political pressure and with fierce determination to stand for the truth, stated that "the weight of testimony shows that none of the soldiers participated in the shooting."

Thus, I began my research from an interest in how my paternal kinsman—grandfather Walter S. Scott—had served with black troops. Then, when I learned of the intersection of my maternal kinsman with the same general subject, I felt even more urgency to bring to light some of the unknown facts about African American soldiers in the earlier history of our nation.

Lord Wellington once said, "At the end of every campaign, truth lies at the bottom of a deep well and it often takes twenty years to get her out." The Spanish-American War is no exception, with the only difference being that it has taken almost one hundred years to bring this aspect of the truth to light. Now, at almost the centennial of the events of that two-week period beginning in late June 1898, it is time to set the record straight and give credit where it is due. With the perspective of almost a century one can see, sandwiched in the darkest period of American racial strife, a few shining days of unequaled heroism by black soldiers that changed the course of American and world history. Black soldiers were particularly outstanding in their devotion to duty, their courage, their discipline, and their determination to win at any cost. Throughout the history of the world, any army would have considered itself fortunate to have had such a collection of military talent.

BIBLIOGRAPHY

"Black Americans and the Quest for Empire; 1898-1903." *Journal of Southern History* 28.

"The Black Volunteers in the Spanish American War." *Military Affairs* 38 (April 1974): 48-53.

Strength for the Fight: A History of Black Americans in the Military. New York: Free Press, 1986.

The Most Famous Soldier in America. Alexandria, Va.: Amchon Publications, 1989.

"When Johnny Went Marching Out." *McClures Magazine* 11 (June 1894).

Aronson, Theodore. *The Crown of Spain.* New York: Bobbs Merrill Co., 1966.

Azay, A.C.M. *Charge: The Story of the Battle of San Juan Hill.* New York: McKay, Longmans, Green, 1961.

Beisner, Robert L. *Twelve Against Empire: The Anti-Imperialists, 1898-1900.* New York: McGraw Hill, 1968.

Bond, Horace Mann. "The Negro in the Armed Forces of the United States Prior to World War I." *Journal of Negro Education* 12 (Summer 1943): 263-267.

Bonsal, Stephen. "The Fight for Santiago; The Story of The Soldiers in the Cuban Campaign From Tampa to Surrender." *Southern Workman,* 28 (August 1898).

———. "The Negro Soldier in War and Peace." *North American Review* 186 (June 1907): 321-27.

Brophy, William S. *The Krag Rifle.* North Hollywood, Ca.: Beinfield Publishers Inc., 1980.

Brown, Charles A. *The Correspondents' War.* New York: Charles Scribner's Sons, 1967.

Carr, Raymond. *Spain 1808-1939.* London: Oxford University Press, 1966.

Carman, W.V. *A History of Firearms.* New York: St. Martin's Press, 1955.

Caruth, Garton. *The Encyclopedia of American Facts and Dates.* New York: Harper and Row Publishers, 1989.

Cashin, H.V. *Under Fire With the Tenth U.S. Calvary.* Salem, N.H.: Ayer Co. Publishers, Inc., 1969.

Churchill, Winston. *My Early Life.* New York: Scribner, 1930.

Churchill, Randolph. *Winston Churchill, Vol. 1.* Boston: Houghton Mifflin Co., 1966.

Coffner, Edward M. *The Old Army.* New York: Oxford University Press, 1986.

Commager, Henry Steele. *Living Ideas in America.* New York: Harper and Brothers Publishers, 1951.

Cosmas, Graham. *An Army for Empire.* Columbia, Mo.: University of Missouri Press, 1971.

Cortez, Hernan. *Address to His Army.* Quoted in *de Gomara, Isotria De La Conquista De Mexico.* 1552.

Cronin, Marcus D. *Historical Sketch of the Twenty-fifth Infantry.* Ft. Bliss, TX.: U.S. Army, 1907.

Dupuy, R.E., and N.H. Baumer. *The Little Wars of the United States.* New York: Hawthorn Books, Inc., 1968.

Faulkner, H.U. *American Political and Social History.* New York: Appleton, Century, Crofts Inc., 1948.

Fletcher, Marvin E. *The Black Soldier and Officer in the United States Army.* Columbia, Missouri: University of Missouri Press, 1974.

Foner, Jack D. *The U.S. Soldier Between Two Wars: 1865-1891.* New York, 1970.

———. *Blacks and the Military in American History.* New York: Praeger, 1974.

Fowler, Arlen L. *The Black Infantry in the West.* Westport, CT: Greenwood Publishing, 1971.

Funston, Frederick. *Memories of Two Wars.* New York: Charles Scribner's Sons, 1914.

Gallagher, K.S., and R.L. Pigeon. *Infantry Regiments Of The United States Army: Decorations And Honors.* New York: Military Press, 1986.

Gatewood, W.B. *Black Americans And The White Man's Burden;1898-1903.* Urbana, IL: University of Illinois Press, 1979.

———. *Smoked Yankees And The Struggle For Empire.* Fayetteville, Ark.: University Of Arkansas Press,1987.

Gatewood, Willard B., Jr. "Negro Troops in Florida, 1898," *Florida Historical Quarterly* 29 (July 1970):1-15.

Gibson, John, M. *Physician to the World: The Life and Times of William L. Gorgas.* Tuscaloosa, Ala.: The University of Alabama Press, 1989.

Glass E.L.N. *The Tenth Cavalry.* Ft. Collins, CO: The Old Army Press, 1927.

Glatthaar, Joseph. *Forged in Battle.* London: The Free Press, Collier Macmillan Publishing,1990.

Goldhurst, Richard. *Pipe, Clay and Drill; John J. Pershing: The Classic American Soldier.* New York: Reader's Digest Press, Thomas J. Crowell Co., 1977.

Harbrough, William, H. *The Life and Times of Theodore Roosevelt.* New York: Oxford University Press, 1978.

Hedren, Paul L. *The Great Sioux War.* Helena, Mon.: Montana Historical Society Press, 1991.

Herner, Charles. *The Arizona Rough Riders.* Tucson, Ariz.: University of Arizona Press, 1970.

Johnson, Edward A. *History of Negro Soldiers in the Spanish-American War.* Raleigh: Capital Publishing Co.,1899.

Johnson, Paul. *The Birth of the Modern.* New York: Harper Collins Publishing, 1991.

Kahn, David. *The Codebreakers.* New York: The McMillan Co., 1968.

Kavaler, Lucy. *The Astors.* Binghamton, N.Y.: Vail Ballou Press, 1966.

Keller, Allen. *The Spanish American War: A Compact History.* New York: Hawthorn Books Inc.,1969.

Kennan, George. *Campaigning in Cuba.* Port Washington, N.Y.: Kennikat Press, 1977.

Kerigan,E. *American Medals and Decorations.* New York: B.D.D. Promotional Book Co., Inc., 1990.

Leckie, William F. *The Buffalo Soldiers: A Narrative of Negro Cavalry in the West.* Norman, OK: University of Oklahoma Press,1967.

Lee, Irvin H. *Negro Medal of Honor Men.* New York: Dodd, Mead, 1967.

Life: Looking Back. New York: Time, Inc., 1992.

Lincoln, W. Bruce. *In Wars Dark Shadow.* New York: Dial Press, 1983.

Lowell, Robert. *For the Union Dead.* New York: American Book - Stratford Press, 1964.

Manchester, William. *The Last Lion, Volume I.* Boston, Mass.: Little, Brown, and Co., 1983.

Martin, Ralph, G. *Jennie: The Life of Lady Randolph Churchill, VOL. 2.* Englewood Cliffs, N. J.: Prentice Hall, 1971.

Mason, S. J.,L.H. Miller, and T. Shiroishi. *British Journal of Hematology*

Mencken, H.L. *The American Language.* New York: A.A. Knopf, 1945.

Millis, Walter. *The Martial Spirit: A Study of Our War with Spain.*
New York: Houghton Mifflin Co., 1931.

Morning Tribune. Tampa, FL.. Various Issues, June 10, 1898-Aug. 13, 1898.

Morris, Edmund. *The Rise of Theodore Roosevelt.* New York: Coward, McCann, and Geoghegan, Inc.1979.

Muller, William G. *The Twenty-fourth Infantry., Past and Present.* n.p.,1923.

New York Times. New York, NY, Various Issues, June 9, 1898-July 3, 1898.

Nally, Bernard C. *Strength for the Fight: A History of Black Americans in the Military.* London: The Free Press, Collier Macmillan Publishers, 1986.

Nankivell, John H. *History of the Twenty-fifth Regiment of the United States Infantry, 1869-1926.* Denver: Smith-Brooks Printing Co., 1927.

North American Review: Vol.186, June 1907, p. 325.

Old Army Press: Buffalo Soldiers West. Ft. Collins, CO.

Old Army Press: The 24th Infantry. Ft. Collins, CO.

O'Toole, G. J. A. *The Spanish War: An American Epic.* New York: W. W. Norton and Co., 1984.

Parker, James. *Rear Admirals Sampson and Schley and Cervera.* New York: The Neal Publishing Co., 1910.

Roosevelt, Theodore. *An Autobiography.* New York: Charles Scribner's Sons, 1926.

Rouse, W.J. "The Colored Regulars." *New York Times Magazine* (June 5, 1898).

Selds, George. *The Great Thoughts.* New York: Ballantine Books, 1985.

Shapiro, Herbert. *White Violence and Black Response.* Amherst: University of Massachusetts Press, 1898.

Smiley, John. *In Cuba with Shafter.* New York:1899.

Smith, Page. *The Nation Comes of Age, Vol. IV.* New York: McGraw Hill Publishers, 1981.

Smyth, Donald. *Guerrilla Warrior: The Early Life of John J. Pershing.* New York: Charles Scribner's Sons, 1973.

Speller, R. J., J. G. Dawson, and T. H. Williams. *Dictionary of American Military Biography.* Westport, Conn.: Greenwood Press, 1984.

Steward, Theophilus G. *Colored Regulars in the United States Army.* Philadelphia: A.M.E. Book Concern, 1904.

Swanberg, W. A. *Citizen Hearst.* New York: Scribner, 1961.

Tocqueville, Alexis De. *Democracy in America.* Garden City, N. J.: Anchor Books, 1969.

Tolstoy, Leo. *War and Peace.* Garden City, N.Y.: Blue Ribbon Books, 1975.

Trask, David. *The War with Spain in 1898.* New York: Macmillan Publishing Co., 1981.

Tsouras, Peter. *Warrior's Words.* New York: Sterling Publishers Inc., 1992.

Urwin, G. J. W. *The United States Cavalry.* New York: Sterling Publishers Inc., 1984.

Utley, Robert. *Frontier Regulars: the United States Army and the Indian; 1866-1891.* New York: Macmillan, 1973.

————. *The Indian Frontier of the American West.* Albuquerque, N.M.: University of New Mexico Press, 1984.

Villard, Oswald G. "The Negro in the Regular Army." *Atlantic Monthly* 81 (June 1903).

Welsh, Douglas. *The History of American Wars.* Greenwich, Conn.: Bison Books, 1983.

Wheeler, J. R. *The Santiago Campaign, 1898.* New York: Lamson, Wolffe and Co.

Whitney, Casper. *Harpers Monthly* (June 1898).

Woodward, C. V. *The Strange Career of Jim Crow.* New York: Oxford University Press, 1966.

Wynes, C. E. *The Negro in the South in 1865.* Tuscaloosa, Ala.: University of Alabama Press, 1965.

Pamphlets

Bureau Development, Inc. *Handbook 118, Part V, Life of the Soldier — Military Routines,* Washington, D.C.:1983, 1990.

Cincinnati Fourteen. *Newsletter of the Society of Cincinnati.* Washington, D.C.: Vol. XXVII, No. 1, Oct. 1991.

May, A.., Huens,E.R. The Mechanism and Prevention of Sickling. British Medical Bulletin, Vol 32: pp. 223-233. 1976.

U.S. Government Documents

Congressional Record. Vols. 84, p.686-688. U.S. Government Printing Office, Washington, D.C.: October 21, 1939.

Senate Doc. 8, Vol. 1, 55-3, 3725.

Senate P. , Vol. 10,1664 56-1, 3895.

Senate Doc. , Vol. 11,15755-33735.

Huston, J.A. Sinews of War. Army Logistics: 1775-1966. U.S. Govertnment Printing Office, 1966.

Kennedy, John F. Public Papers of the Presidents of the United States: 1961.

Matlof, Maurice. American Military History: U.S. Army; C.M.H. Pub. 30-1,1985.

Utley, Robert. Fort Davis National Historic Site, Texas. National Park Service, Handbook 38, 1965.

NOTES

1   Dissatisfaction with the obsolete .45 caliber rifle which the American army had used for years motivated the purchase of the Swedish Krag-Jorgensen rifle, which not only had a longer range but fired a small caliber bullet at greater speed. Approximately 20,000 of the new rifles were delivered to the army in 1895. In 1903 American production of the weapon began at the Springfield Armory in Massachusetts.

2   In 1866 more than two thousand ex-slaves had been recruited for the armed forces from New Orleans. Criteria for selection were that only the largest, most powerful and blackest Negroes were to be accepted. These were the men who formed the core troops of the Twenty-fourth and Twenty-fifth Infantry Regiments as well as of the Ninth and Tenth Cavalries.

3   One reason that desertion was so common was that there was an 80 percent chance of never being retaken in spite of pursuit and rewards offered by the Army to civilians that might lead to recapture. If caught, the deserting soldier was harshly disciplined, and, until 1870, a small "O" was branded on the left buttock as part of the punishment.

4   The revolutionists were following the example set by blacks in Haiti at the beginning of the century when they had defeated French rulers and gained autonomy over part of the island of Santa Domingo (now called Hispaniola). At that time there were some 500,000 slaves and 50,000 white French residents on the western one-third of the island, which became the nation of Haiti. Added to this were the 30,000 freedmen ("affranchis"), freed slaves, who had given their support to the revolting slaves. The Cuban revolution taken up by the descendants of slaves was thus yet another phase of blacks' long struggle for freedom, respect, equality, dignity, honor, and political power in the New World. The Cuban rebellion brought worldwide sympathy for the insurgents, but not every observer was sympathetic. Young Winston Churchill visited Cuba in 1895 as a war correspondent under the aegis of Spain to report on conditions among the rebels. Openly contemptuous of the disorganized, ineffective, cruel manner in which the rebels conducted their unsuccessful campaign, Churchill stated that their army, which consisted to a large extent of black men, was an undisciplined rabble. In Cuba on November 30, 1895, his twenty-first birthday, Winston Churchill heard for the first time, "shots fired in anger and bullets strike flesh or whistle through the air." This occurred when a small group of rebels attacked him and a few Spaniards while swimming, and was the first of many occasions in which enemy fire was directed at Churchill.

5   As a child, Roosevelt had been sickly and several times was on the point of death from asthma. He stated in his autobiography that two of his earliest memories were of his father holding him in his arms at night and walking with him, and and of sitting

up in bed gasping, with his mother and father trying to help him. By adulthood, however, he had become a paragon of robustness. His physical courage was beyond question, as was demonstrated once while he was a rancher in North Dakota. In the dead of winter, three bandits stole a boat belonging to Roosevelt. With two friends, he built a replacement boat and set out in pursuit in below-freezing weather. Leaving some six days after the theft, they floated down the Little Missouri River in temperatures as low as zero degrees, fighting through ice floes and killing game for food. Three harrowing days later they captured the thieves and retrieved the stolen boat but then faced a quandary. As was the custom in that part of the country, most ranchers would have shot or hanged the culprits on the spot, but Roosevelt decided to take them to the nearest sheriff for due process of law, which required a brutal eight-day trek across frozen prairie. For his efforts he received a fee of fifty dollars, part for making the arrests and part for the three hundred miles traveled.

6   Spanish intelligence-gathering and communications were even worse. Even by late June, a portion of the Spanish empire was not even aware that war had been declared. While the American invasion fleet was still at sea off Cuba, the U.S.S. *Clarkson* steamed into the harbor at Guam and fired a volley at the town. The Spanish commander, not knowing that war had been declared between the two countries, sent a message of apology to the American captain for not having returned his salute. He confessed that his inability to do so was because he had no ammunition on the island. Discovered by Ferdinand Magellan, Guam, the first Spanish possession in the Pacific, was surrendered to the Americans on June 20, 1898, and has remained an American possession to this date.

7   Seeing the great need to protect communications from other countries as well as from his political opponents, Thomas Jefferson, either while secretary of state from 1790 to 1793 or while vice-president from 1797 to 1800, invented a wheel cipher. This code machine was by far the most advanced of its day. He seems to have invented it somewhat casually, rather than after great thought and study of the history and techniques of cryptography. He had so little appreciation of the real breakthrough he himself had achieved in the specialty of cryptography that he recommended to Secretary of State James Madison another code machine invented by a friend, Dr. Robert Patterson, then president of the American Philosophical Society. The second model was used by the State Department for many years but was in no way as sophisticated and impenetrable as Jefferson's. Jefferson's invention was discovered among his papers in the Library of Congress in 1922, the year in which the army adopted an almost identical device invented by someone else. Other branches of the government used the Jefferson device that resisted the best efforts of twentieth century cryptanalysts to break its code. It was used by the navy at least through 1968; so Jefferson is truly the father of American cryptography.

8   A few of these volunteers, however, were indeed chosen to fill out the ranks of regular military outfits to bring them up to strength. Even though the volunteers selected had serious deficiencies in military training and experience this was deemed

a wise move. Two famous Civil War generals wrote pertinent comments about the value of mixing new recruits with seasoned regular soldiers. General of the Army William T. Sherman wrote: "I believe that five hundred new men added to an old and experienced regiment were more valuable than a thousand men in the form of a new regiment, for the former, by association with good, experienced captains, lieutenants, and non-commissioned officers, soon became veterans, whereas the latter were generally unavailable for a year." General Grant echoed this: "The citizen soldiers were associated with so many disciplined men and professionally educated officers that, when they went into engagements, it was with a confidence they would not have felt otherwise. They became soldiers themselves almost at once."

9   When the Spanish colonized Central and South America they had planned on using Indians as slave labor. However, many Indians were chronically infected with Vivax malaria, an endemic tropical disease that is widespread in South America, the Caribbean, North America, and West Africa, although other even more virulent forms are found in all subtropical and tropical areas of the world. Indians already affected with malaria were especially susceptible to the other contagious diseases the Spanish had brought to the New World, and many Indians died. But many west Africans had a genetic immunity, linked to the sickle cell trait, to Vivax malaria. The gene that protected them from endemic malaria made them more suitable as laborers in the western hemisphere than the native Indians. Therefore, slave ships started bringing Africans to the Caribbean to replace Indian labor. It is fascinating to speculate on how history might have been different but for this genetic circumstance. If west Africans had not seemed so healthy as a result of their genetic trait, slavery might not have thrived, since the expense involved in transporting a labor force no healthier than that already on site would have made slavery uneconomical, and slavery probably never would have involved the numbers reached in the seventeenth through the nineteenth centuries and might not have existed at all. (In 1811, when a weakened Spain was considering some sort of proportional representation in its government, it estimated that there were in the Indies seventeen million people, of whom three million were white, four million black, and ten million Indian.)

10   General Nelson A. Miles, born on a farm to a family with no social standing or wealth, had not received a university education, yet he had risen to the highest position in the United States Army. He had acquired very loyal friends among the military hierarchy while serving in the Army during the Civil War, in which he became a major general at the age of twenty-five. He had used his friendships with Generals Grant, Hancock, Sheridan, and Meade to good advantage in the postwar years (Miles had married the daughter of General Sherman). Unfortunately for his future political prospects, he had been in command of Fortress Monroe immediately after the Civil War and thus had become the jailer of Jefferson Davis. Shortly after incarcerating Jefferson Davis, Miles received instructions from Secretary of War Charles A. Dana to put manacles on the hands and feet of his prisoner, to prevent escape in case friends tried a rescue attempt. Davis resisted the placing of manacles on

his extremities, knocking one man down in the process; however, after being overcome by four men, he was finally shackled. The strong-willed Varina Howell Davis, made furious by this treatment of her husband, wrote to national newspapers about this vicious treatment, stating that her husband's health was sinking. So widespread was the publicity about Miles, which included two chapters about him in a book written by Mrs. Davis, that his political prospects were permanently ruined in the South. This doomed his bid for the presidential nomination in 1904. President Theodore Roosevelt later told the editor of *Harper's Weekly* that Miles had approached him several years previously and asked Roosevelt to join him on the next presidential ballot to oppose McKinley. This was at a time when the war in the Philippines was at its most violent stage and while Miles was commanding general of the army. Miles had told Roosevelt that to discredit McKinley he really hoped that America would not win the war in the Philippines. Roosevelt never forgave Miles for his selfish attitude, his conflict of interest, and his lack of dedication to his job of winning the war.

11   Those companies of the Twenty-fifth Infantry sent to Key West became involved in a disgraceful racial episode. Because a corporal and an enlisted man had been jailed, charged with assault with intent to murder, forty armed and uniformed soldiers assaulted the jail at midnight. As a precursor of post-war violent acts, they overpowered the sheriff, smashed the jail, and liberated their comrades.

12   According to H. L. Mencken, the word Jim Crow was first noted by the *Dictionary of the American English* in 1838, stating that "Jim Crow" was a hymn of great antiquity. A song for dancing, "Jim Crow," was written in 1832 by Thomas D. Rice, and the phrase "to jump Jim Crow" appeared shortly thereafter. Jim Crow had become an adjective by 1838 and was used as such in *Uncle Tom's Cabin* by Harriet Beecher Stowe. From that time, the use of the word as an adjective became more common, such as Jim Crow car (1861), Jim Crow school (1903), Jim Crow bill (1904), Jim Crow law (1904), and Jim Crow regulations (1910). Regarding the origins of Jim Crow as a body of regulations restricting and controlling the lives of the black race, many experts state explicitly that the system was born in the North and reached an advanced age before moving South in force. Even Alexis de Tocqueville, writing about America before the Civil War, commented that nowhere are the citizens more intolerant of the black race than in "those states where servitude has never been known." Nevertheless, from the 1870's to the 1960's, segregation was the law and the custom in the Southern states. For example, segregation in public schools started in 1868 in North Carolina, and, in 1876, the legislature made it "legal" by putting the segregation provision in the state's constitution.

13   A reporter who had visited Santiago, Cuba, earlier that year called it "the most unhealthful abode in the Antilles." He stated that not only was it supplied with bad water but, being shut off by mountains from the northern breezes, was suffocatingly hot at all times.

14 Hobson was captured by the Spanish, but the Americans were optimistic that he and his men could be exchanged. The Tampa *Morning Tribune* of June 10, 1898, stated that the commander of the battleship Iowa had sent a truce party as near as possible to the sunken *Merrimac,* under protection of American guns, to negotiate the exchange of Hobson and his men for Spanish prisoners being held in jail in Atlanta: one first lieutenant, seven second lieutenants, one sergeant, and nine privates. Negotiations failed, so Hobson spent the balance of the war in a Santiago prison, situated where he could see at a distance the Battle of San Juan Hill. There was much concern in Washington as to the exact location of Hobson's prison, because it was feared that he might be in the line of fire if the Americans decided to bombard the Spanish fleet and Santiago. Secretary Long even obtained a Senate resolution directing the navy to find out whether Hobson was in the line of fire. On June 30, the day before the Battle of San Juan Hill, Hobson's spirits rose when he spied an American observation balloon. Hobson and his men were released in a prisoner swap on July 6, two days after the Spanish fleet was destroyed outside Santiago harbor.

15 The Spanish had their own mule problems. Early in June 1898, a mule buyer, Lorenzo, was apprehended buying large quantities of the pack animals at Fort Smith, Arkansas. At a mule auction, a note written in Spanish had dropped from his pocket. When translated, the note proved to be an incriminating secret communication from a Lieutenant Caranzo, the Spanish agent in Montreal, Canada. Lorenzo was lynched on the spot.

16 In 1615, Miguel Cervantes, in Don Quixote, commented on artillery: "Blessed be those happy ages that were strangers to the dreadful fury of these devilish instruments of artillery, whose inventor, I am satisfied, is now in hell, receiving the reward of his cursed invention, which is the cause that very often a cowardly base hand takes away the life of the bravest gentleman."

17 In 1862, Dr. Gatling of North Carolina developed the machine gun named after him. This gun had four to ten rifled barrels that were rotated around a central axis by means of a crank. Bullets were continuously fed by gravity through a trough, and the gun fired as long as the crank was turned. Although early models were liable to jam, later electrically driven models, could fire 3600 rounds a minute. The Hotchkiss gun was also a weapon in the American arsenal and was to prove very effective in the Battle of Las Guasimas. Like the Gatling gun, it could fire over 600 rounds a minute, and, using larger and more explosive shells, could inflict more damage. Invented by an American living in Paris, the Hotchkiss gun had a single barrel and an escape port to force gases to drive the breech action, the loading and the shell ejection.

18 The Spanish had displayed extreme brutality toward the native Cuban population and frequently had used torture and other harsh methods to bring them under control. General Weyler, known as "the butcher," had developed concentration camps in Cuba in which masses of the peasant population were confined (causing thirty thousand to die of disease and starvation). This was forty years before the Nazis

used similar enclosures for civilians, but just a few years before their use by the British in the Boer War, when General Kitchener penned thousands of Boer women and children in concentration camps, where more than twenty thousand died. General Weyler had created his concentration camps to control the native population of Cuba and deny the rebels support from the towns and countryside. In his effort to trap his opponents in limited areas of the island he had constructed the tropical equivalent of a nineteenth century Berlin Wall, a clearing up to two hundred yards wide, extending across the width of the island. This clearing, called a "trocha," was completely obstructed on each side by trees that had been felled in creating the clearing. Such trees, laid in parallel rows on each side, formed a dense wall-like barrier higher than a man's head, through which a horse could not pass and a man only with great difficulty. Between the walls of felled trees was a military railroad, a string of small and large forts, and land mines. Weyler constructed one such barrier, fifty miles long, to confine the insurgents at the eastern end of the island. A second barrier at the western end of Cuba effectively contained the forces of rebel leader Maceo.

19 Prominent black Americans later argued that because Negro soldiers had made efficient commanders under combat conditions, they should qualify as candidates for commissions in the regular Army, but such would not be the case for many years. Following the battles in Cuba, General Thomas A. Morgan addressed the issue of promoting blacks to officer status and possibly admitting blacks to West Point. He stated that officers were the most exclusive class in the Army and formed an elite group among themselves, considering themselves gentlemen. He thought that blacks should be included in this group, stating: "With my experience in command of 5,000 Negro soldiers (in the Civil War), I would, on the whole, prefer, I think, the command of a corps of Negro troops to that of a corps of white troops. With the magnificent record of their fighting qualities on many a hard-contested field, it is not unreasonable to ask that a still further opportunity be extended them in commissioning them as officers as well as enlisting them as soldiers."

20 When his captain was wounded in the initial attack at Las Guasimas, Bowman became one of the first black non-commissioned officers to lead troops in battle in this war.

21 An occasional visitor to Shafter's tent was John Jacob Astor IV, in Cuba because of his determination to participate in the war. Initially appointed by Theodore Roosevelt as an inspector-general of the Navy, with the outbreak of hostilities he had been given the rank of lieutenant colonel as an inspector of Army camps in the United States. On being transferred to Cuba, he witnessed the Battle of Santiago. He contracted malaria and was discharged, but had reached the rank of colonel.

22 It is probable that Wheeler had suffered his first attack of the endemic tertian malaria, characterized by prostration and violent shaking chills and fever, symptoms that invariably subside within a few hours. The victim feels perfectly normal the following day, only to have an identical recurrence of the severe symptoms every

other day thereafter until treatment is started.

23   Although barbed wire was patented in 1867, the first practical machinery for its manufacture was not invented until 1890, after which its use for demarcating cattle ranges in the West ended the open range. Military strategists had found it an ideal supplement to perimeter defenses, so its use for this purpose spread so rapidly that by 1903 the generals of the Russian Army were severely criticized for not laying in a supply of barbed wire to aid in the defense of Port Arthur during the Russo-Japanese War.

24   Disobedience of orders from a commanding officer is in keeping with the actions of famous generals and admirals throughout history. In 1801, at the Battle of Copenhagen, Admiral Nelson received a signal from the ship of his commander-in-chief that instructed him to leave off action and retire from the battle. Stating that he had one blind eye, Nelson told his subordinate that he had a right to be blind sometimes; so, putting his false eye in front of his good eye, he exclaimed, "I really do not see the signal." Then he continued the battle to a successful conclusion.

25   Creelman, a veteran of his trade, had traveled worldwide and interviewed such people as the Pope, Henry Stanley, Sitting Bull, Count Tolstoy, and the Spanish General Weyler, as well as having covered action in the Sino-Japanese and the Greco-Turkish Wars.

26   Prior to the war, the famous sculptor and painter, Frederic Remington, had asked Hearst about the possibilities of creating satisfactory paintings of war scenes. Hearst reassured him in his usual arrogant manner; "You create the paintings, and I'll create the war."

27   General Chaffee was the only one of all the commanding officers who had not spent a portion of his regimental years with black troops.

28   In a commonplace comment regarding the type of work that black troops were required to perform wherever stationed, even in Cuba, Colonel Joseph Haskitt of the 17th Infantry said, "Our colored troops are 100 percent superior to the Cubans. He is a good scout, brave soldier and, not only that, he is everywhere to be seen building roads for the movement of heavy guns."

29   Military historians have noted that technological improvements developed during one war are frequently not decisive in that war, but, after further improvement, are frequently essential to victory in the following war. Aerial reconnaissance in the Spanish- American War was innovative in using the skies for surveillance, but, while helpful, it did not prove essential to the success of American arms in the war. The development of the tank by the British in World War I has a similar history. The availability of tanks came too late to be of much help in assuring Allied victory in the war , but tanks did prove their effectiveness in breaking through fixed barbed wire and trenches, thereby making trench warfare obsolete in the next war. Pointing to the Battle of Cambrai, in which British tanks had been very effective late in the First World War, Churchill railed against the stupidity of Allied generals in not using

tanks earlier in the war, stating they "had been content to fight machine-gun bullets with the breasts of gallant men, and think that was waging war."

30 In 1780, George Washington wrote Congress on his feelings about volunteer troops: "No militia will ever acquire the habits necessary to resist a regular force . . . The firmness requisite for the real business of fighting is only to be attained by a constant course of discipline and service. I have never yet been witness to a single instance that can justify a different opinion, and it is most to be wished that the liberties of America may no longer be trusted, in any material degree, to so precarious a dependence." In a later time, Winston Churchill wrote, "Wars are not won by heroic militia." In the case of the 71st New York Volunteers, it seems beyond question that the untested soldiers did break under the initial onslaught of Spanish fire. Examination of statistics presented after the battle by General Wheeler indicates a very low casualty rate among the New Yorkers, in comparison with other units. Of the 43 officers present for duty on July 1, only one was wounded, and of the 915 enlisted men, only 13 were killed and 59 wounded. This is about half the casualty rate of the other outfits. Of particular interest are the 43 officers and enlisted men reported missing (deserted?) after the action; the largest number in any other unit was five. Stephen Crane, author of *The Red Badge of Courage*, was among the many reporters in Cuba. Crane's dispatch to his newspaper impugning the valor of the 71st caused an angry reaction in New York, where many leading citizens had sons in the unit. Crane was a reporter for *The World*, a Joseph Pulitzer paper; so naturally the Hearst paper, *The Journal*, took the opposite side of the angry debate. In an effort to make amends for the harm done to the reputations of the young soldiers of the state, *The World* raised funds from the public for a memorial to the Seventy-first Infantry. The men of the regiment refused to accept the memorial, so the money was returned.

31 General George S. Patton Jr. has described this type of fighting: "Battle is an orgy of disorder. No level lawns or marker flags exist to aid us strut ourselves in vain display, but rather groups of weary wandering men seek gropingly for means to kill their foe. The sudden change from accustomed order, to utter disorder, to chaos, but emphasizes the folly of schooling to precision and obedience where only fierceness and habitual disorder are useful."

32 While at West Point as tactical officer, Pershing became very unpopular with the administration and especially with the cadets—in fact they grew to hate him. On learning that he had served with a black outfit (Tenth Cavalry), they started calling him "Nigger Jack," later changed to "Black Jack." Intent on gaining battle experience in the war, Pershing had used his considerable influence to rejoin the Tenth Cavalry in April 1898, and had been assigned duties as regimental quartermaster.

33 Henry Shrapnel, an English artillery officer, developed an artillery shell containing musket balls. These shells, later known as shrapnel, were first put into use in 1803.

34 Despite his panache, Roosevelt's command inexperience was evident on several occasions. Because he was the one person who achieved the most personal benefit

from the war with Spain, it is worth noting a few of his major mistakes: In the Battle of Las Guasimas, his company was deployed in an attacking line by orders of Colonel Wood. Without notifying his regimental commander, Roosevelt moved his troops to a new position, leaving a gap in the attacking line. The regiment luckily escaped tragedy from this bit of individual initiative, but it did bring forth some strong words from his commanding officer. On the summit of Kettle Hill, Roosevelt charged down the hill with his troops, but had failed to be certain that his non-commissioned officers and soldiers were aware of his plan. Since only a few had heard his command, most were left behind, and Roosevelt gallantly charged forward leading a paltry pack of brave cavalrymen. When he had returned to the summit to retrieve the balance of his troops he was no longer the ranking officer, since General Sumner had arrived. He then had to ask permission to make another charge down the hill with his full body of troops. For veteran officers it was a novel sight to see a lieutenant colonel, commander of a whole regiment, leading a small contingent of men down the hill into a hail of bullets. With seeming exhilaration, a short time later, he charged up the slope of San Juan Hill, acting more like a platoon leader or a company commander than a regimental commander. Thus, one could summarize the military style of Roosevelt as one who gallantly led_but did not command. In enthusiasm, physical stamina, and willingness to brave enemy fire in the open, Roosevelt was very much like his contemporary young Winston Churchill; however he lacked the military education of Churchill (a graduate of Sandhurst) and, consequently, let his animal spirits prevail over orthodox military conduct. After the Battle of San Juan Hill, in recapitulating events, Roosevelt stated that, when he had reached the trenches on the summit of San Juan Heights, he found them "filled with dead bodies in the light blue and white uniform of the Spanish regular army...most of the fallen had little holes in their heads from which their brains were oozing; for they were covered from their neck down by the trenches." At least two participants later reported that no trenches had existed in that area. Colonel Alexander Bacon of the 21st New York Volunteers made this acerbic comment: "These trenches, being, then, imaginary, it is fair to argue that they were filled with imaginary dead Spaniards."

35   Inspired by the remarkable courage of the 10th Cavalry, the New York Journal commented: "The two most picturesque and most characteristically American commands in General Shafter's army bore off the great honors of a day in which all won honor. No man can read the story in today's Journal of the Rough Rider's charge on San Juan Hill, of Theodore Roosevelt's mad daring in the face of what seemed certain death, without having his pulses beat faster and some reflected light of the proud battle gleam from his eyes. And over against this scene of the cowboy and the college graduate, the New York man-about-town, and Arizona badman, united in one coherent war machine, set the picture of the 10th United States Cavalry—the famous colored regiment." "Side-by-side with Roosevelt's men they fought—these black men. Scarce used to freedom themselves, they are dying that Cuba may be free. 'Their marksmanship was magnificent' say the eyewitnesses. 'Their courage was

superb.' They bore themselves like veterans and gave proof positive that, out of nature's naturally peaceful, careless and playful, military discipline and an inspiring cause can make soldiers worthy to rank with Caesar's legions or Cromwell's army. The Rough Riders and the black regiments: in those two commands is an epitome of almost our whole national character." A young Rough Rider named Frank Knox, who later became Secretary of the Navy under Franklin D. Roosevelt, became separated from his outfit while it was charging up San Juan Hill. Like many others who become separated from their units, he joined the nearest body of men and continued to advance. Knox joined the black 10th Cavalry soldiers who were also moving forward in the advance. He later wrote home: "I must say that I never saw braver men anywhere. Some of those who rushed up the hill will live in my memory forever."

36   Three days after the battle an American newspaper wrote: "All honors to the black troops of the gallant Tenth. No more striking example of bravery and coolness has been shown since the destruction of the *Maine* than by the colored veterans of the 10th Cavalry during the attack on San Juan Hill on Saturday." "By the side of the intrepid Rough Riders, they followed their leader up the terrible hill from whose crest the desperate Spaniards poured down a deadly fire of shell and musketry. They never faltered. The gaps in their ranks were filled as soon as made. Firing as they marched, their aim was splendid, their coolness was superb and their courage aroused the admiration of their comrades. Their advance was greeted with wild cheers from the white regiments, and with an answering shout they pressed onward and over the trenches they had taken, in close pursuit of the retreating enemy. The war has not shown greater heroism. The men whose own freedom was baptized with blood have proved themselves to be capable of giving up their lives that others may be free. Today is a glorious Fourth for all races in this great land."

37   A soldier of the white 17th Infantry gave his testimony: "I shall never forget the lst of July. At one time in the engagement of that day the 2lst Infantry had faced a superior force of Spaniards and were almost completely surrounded. The 24th Infantry of colored troops, seeing the perilous position of the 2lst, rushed to the rescue, charged and routed the enemy, thereby saving the ill-fated regiment." Equally heroic and impressive was the performance of the 24th Infantry on the extreme left of the American line in the attack on the Spanish stronghold at San Juan Hill. One black infantrymen who participated in the storming of San Juan Heights, under a barrage of Spanish bullets, described his colleagues as "an angry mob who were oblivious to the death and the destruction around them." When many officers were either killed or wounded, noncommissioned officers took charge of the battle, but there was really no formal organization of the troops. In this disorder of the San Juan assault the performance of the black noncommissioned officers was extremely effective. A Captain in the 71st New York Volunteers declared that the black Twenty-fourth Infantry did more than any other to win the day at San Juan: "As they charged up through the white soldiers their enthusiasm spread, and the entire line fought the

better for their cheers and their wild rush."

38 Baker reached the rank of captain and served with distinction with the 49th Volunteers in the war in the Philippines. His company had 106 men on its rolls, none of whom lost a day of service due to illness during the course of one year. Even more striking is that during that period none of the men went before a court-martial, a record far superior to that of any white company.

39 During the Civil War, Congress had seen the need to establish a medal for heroism in battle. The first such medal, the Navy Medal of Honor, was authorized in December 1861, but its usefulness was limited by its specific Civil War motif. About six months later, an Army Medal of Honor was created by a resolution of Congress and signed into law by Abraham Lincoln, and this medal served as the only award for heroism until 1918. The medal was redesigned twice, in 1896 and in 1904, continuing to be the only award for heroism until the "Pyramid of Honor" was created in 1918, establishing awards for varying degrees of heroism.

40 Although reasonable and humane, the final agreement to send home the Spanish Army and their families at the expense of the United States proved to be costly. The Secretary of War, in February 1899, persuaded Congress to appropriate $1,500,000 to help with the costs, but this proved far too little, so another $8,500,000 was added a month later. When even more bills started coming in for the costs related to sending home the families and soldiers from the Philippines, Congress, in January 1900, added another $750,000 to that already spent.

41 Within little more than a month after the battle, both Sampson and Schley received significant promotions in rank. Sampson advanced eight places in rank and moved from acting rear admiral to the rank of rear admiral. Schley, who had previously outranked Sampson, also became a rear admiral, but, since he was advanced only six places now found himself one rank lower than Sampson. The injustice rankled, and most of the nation and newspapers took the side of Admiral Schley. There was a striking difference between the treatment accorded Admiral Nelson of the British Navy after his unique role in the victory, in 1797, at the Battle of St. Vincent, over the Spanish fleet off the coast of Portugal, and that given Commodore Schley by his commanding officer, Admiral Sampson. Nelson, who was only a Commodore at the time, had deliberately disobeyed his admiral's orders by changing the order of battle during the period of heaviest fighting, a tactic that won the battle. When firing had ceased, Nelson was welcomed aboard the flagship with cheers and greeted effusively by Admiral Sir John Jervis, who allowed him to keep his captured Spanish sword. In dramatic contrast, Schley was greeted with coolness when he went aboard Admiral Sampson's ship and, furthermore, was directed to change the contents of the first telegram he had sent announcing victory.

42 In the 20th century weapons have become much more effective killers of men, so the Spanish-American War was among the last wars in which the mortality from disease exceeded that due to arms. After this war weapons took center-stage in their

killing capacities, leaving parasites and bacteria a secondary role. Knowledge of the mode of transmission of yellow fever when coupled with proper sanitary practices, learned during and shortly after the Spanish-American War, enabled subsequent armies to drastically lower their death rates from disease. Previously, those wars fought in temperate and tropical regions sometimes had death rates from disease often as high as forty times that from battlefield injuries.

43 It is unfortunate that after all of her work and suffering Miss Barton did not receive adequate national or international recognition. Lena P. Cowley, who had stayed home in New York to organize Red Cross affairs, received very extensive post-war praise and was awarded the Medal of Honor by Congress on March 1, 1899. On the recommendation of Secretary of War, R. A. Alger, the award was given for her efforts toward coordinating the supply of Red Cross nurses to Cuba and Puerto Rico.

44 In studying the Spanish-American War and its deadly aftermath of disease, I was intrigued by the role played by William Gorgas, who has always been a hero to the medical profession. One of his subordinates, Dr. Lloyd Noland, a close friend of my father's, eventually settled in Birmingham and became a pillar of strength in the medical community as well as a leading citizen of the city. A few years after the war, Gorgas, an Alabama native, was instrumental not only in controlling yellow fever, but he also promulgated public heath regulations relating to the control of many tropical diseases.

45 More friction developed between Roosevelt and Secretary Alger following a letter sent by Roosevelt requesting that he, all his troops, and the troops of the regular cavalry be sent to Puerto Rico. The letter, sent on July 23, 1898, stated that the Rough Riders were three times as good as any State troops. He stated further that if the contingent of 1,800 men were sent they would be "worth easily any 10,000 National Guards armed with black powder, Springfield or any other archaic weapon." Undoubtedly incensed over so arrogant a letter, Secretary Alger replied in part: "I suggest that unless you want to spoil the effects and glory of your victory, you make no invidious comparisons. The Rough Riders are no better than other volunteers. They had an advantage in their arms, for which they ought to be very grateful." After the war, Alger, evidently fed up with Roosevelt's arrogance , refused to recommend him to Congress for a Medal of Honor. So unbounded was Roosevelt's political ambition and so determined was he to further his political career that he violated all standards of personal conduct in his efforts to be awarded the medal. He wrote many letters on his own behalf and reinforced his pleading by requesting affidavits testifying to his heroism from those involved in the Battle of San Juan Hill. Roosevelt implored his best friend, Senator Henry Cabot Lodge, to finagle endorsement of his heroism from the War Department, but Alger refused, and the coveted medal for heroism remained forever out of reach. Ironically, twenty-five years after Roosevelt's death at the age of sixty, his oldest son, Brigadier General Theodore Roosevelt, Jr., was awarded a posthumous Medal of Honor for bravery during the Allied D-Day invasion of the Normandy beaches.

46 Thomas Jefferson wrote a friend on June 11, 1807, about his personal attitude toward newspapers: "Nothing can now be believed which is seen in a newspaper. Truth itself becomes suspicious by being put in that polluted vehicle."

47 The attitude of black regular Army soldiers in their desire to show white Americans that, although of a different race, they were capable of battlefield valor equal to that of any race, is reminiscent of the fierce desire of the Japanese-American soldiers in the Second World War. Oriental Americans wanted to show a suspicious and prejudiced nation that they too were loyal citizens and willing to die for their country. About 4000 Japanese-Americans made up the 442nd Regimental Combat Team of the 100th Infantry Battalion, which distinguished itself in the Italian campaign. Because of their determination and bravery these Americans suffered an enormous percentage of casualties.

48 Correspondence between Hearst and President McKinley was released, revealing that Hearst had earlier offered to recruit, train and equip a full regiment of cavalry at his own expense, the only contingency being that Hearst serve in the regiment, either as commander or as a soldier in the ranks. McKinley had refused the offer. The persistent Mr. Hearst then offered to the government his steam yacht, *Buccaneer*, under the condition that he be appointed in command or, at least, second in command. His last offer was accepted by the Secretary of the Navy Allen, so Hearst made preparations for the final step by turning the boat over to the Navy, which he did in Tampa Bay. It was for this reason that military personnel had been discovered on the boat by reporters of the *New York Herald.*

49 The handsome Davis had once been selected by Charles Dana Gibson to pose as a model for photographs with the famed Gibson Girl. William Randolph Hearst had employed Davis as a war correspondent to report on events in Cuba, and Davis certainly proved to be a valuable employee, especially when he participated in the charge up San Juan Hill.

50 On the day before the surrender ceremonies at which the American flag was to be raised in Santiago, a group of correspondents requested that they be allowed to witness the formalities. Shafter emphatically stated that they would not be allowed to enter the city. Asked if they would be allowed in the city a few days later, Shafter again said no, and further indicated that, no matter how long they stayed in Cuba, they would not be allowed to enter the city. Some reporters then made plans to leave Cuba, but a large number remained and sneaked into the city, reporting on the proceedings in spite of Shafter's threat to place them in irons if caught. During the surrender ceremonies a reporter who had climbed to the top of a building in Santiago to witness the raising of the American flag was ordered to come down immediately by General Shafter, incensed by what he considered to be arrogant conduct. The reporter did descend from the building and, on accosting the general, protested the order. The confrontation became so heated that the reporter struck the general with his fist and was placed under immediate arrest. He was soon sent home in disgrace, a mild

punishment considering that he struck a general in time of war.

51 As regards the Brownsville Affair, justice was finally achieved in 1972, when the Army conducted a new investigation of the matter and ordered the penalties rescinded, although by this time all the soldiers involved had died except Dorsey Willis, then 86 years old. The reversal was spurred by a book by John D. Weaver, who after carefully reviewing the evidence argued for exoneration of the soldiers. No provision was made for back pay or other compensation, but Congress, in a burst of generosity, passed a resolution granting the aged Willis $25,000 and eligibility for Veterans Administration hospital benefits.

Index